AF795118

Reluctant Partners Coming Together?
Interface between People, Government and the NGOs

About the Editors

D. Rajasekhar is an Associate Professor (Economics), Decentralisation and Develop-ment Unit, at the Institute for Social and Economic Change, Bangalore. He is currently directing a World Bank funded research project on Roles of Rural Local Organisations in Development Projects. His recent books are '*Decentralised Government and NGOs : Issues, Strategies and Ways Forward*, and '*Poverty Alleviation Strategies of NGOs*'.

R.R. Biradar is a faculty member in the department of Economics at Karnatak University, Dharwad. Previously, he worked at the Centre for Multi-Disciplinary Develop-ment Research, Dharwad, and the Institute for Social and Economic Change, Bangalore, on various issues relating to agriculture, rural non-farm sector, social development, Non-Governmental Organi-sations and Panchayat Raj Institutions.

Reluctant Partners Coming Together?

Interface between People, Government and the NGOs

Edited by

D. Rajasekhar
R. R. Biradar

CONCEPT PUBLISHING COMPANY, NEW DELHI-110059

All rights reserved. No part of this work may be reproduced, stored in a retrieval system, or transmitted in any form or by any means, electronic, mechanical, photocopying, microfilming, recording or otherwise, without the prior written permission of the copyright owner and the publisher.

ISBN : 81-8069-108-X

First Published 2004

© D. Rajasekhar (*b.* 1960)
R. R. Biradar (*b.* 1968)

Published and Printed by
Ashok Kumar Mittal
Concept Publishing Company
A/15-16, Commercial Block, Mohan Garden
New Delhi-110059 (India)

Phones : 25351460, 25351794
Fax : 901-11-25357103
Email : publishir g@conceptpub.com

Acknowledgements

The book brings out the revised papers presented in the two workshops, first, on "Interface between Government Agencies and the Target Group of NGOs" during January 21-23, 1999 at ASRC Centre, Hyderabad; and the second, on "Relucant Partners Revisited : Interface between the Government, NGOs and People" during August 26-27, 1999 at the Institute for Social and Economic Change, Bangalore. The workshops were a product of collective effort by ISEC, Bangalore, Development Support Initiative, Bangalore, GTZ/SHF, Bangalore and IC-NGO Programme, Hyderabad. We place our heartfelt thanks to the then heads of these institutions for their help and support. We would like to thank the participants of the workshops for their active participation and helpful comments.

The idea of conducting the workshops and coming up with a volume was first provided by Ms. Gabrielle Ramm, Team Leader, SHPAP, New Delhi. She remained in touch with the entire process of holding the workshops, and has been a great source of inspiration. In conducting the workshops and preparing the volume for the publication, we have received generous help and support from Mr. V. S. Parthasarathy, Mrs. Namerta, Dr. G. Sridhar, Mr. M. K. Bhat, Mr. N. L. Narasimha Reddy, Ms. G. Sudha and Mr. T. A. Verghese. Our heartfelt thanks to these well meaning friends.

We should also like to place on record the assistance and hospitality offered by the NGOs and SHG members during our field visits for data collection.

Our heartfelt thanks are also due to Dr. M. Govinda Rao, former Director, ISEC, for his encouragement and support in bringing out the volume. We also thank Dr. R. S. Deshpande, Head, ADRT Unit, ISEC, Bangalore for his critical comments and suggestions during the workshop. We would like to sincerely thank Dr. V. M. Rao, Professor Emeritus, ISEC, Bangalore for his comments and suggestions, some of which have played a considerable role in preparing Chapter 2 of the volume.

We are also thankful to Ms. Shobana, Dr. Pushpa Rani, Mr. N. Krishne Gowda and Ms. Shanthi for their efforts and help in conducting the fieldwork, writing the papers and organising the workshops both at Hyderabad and Bangalore, and also Ms. R. Manjula for her support in bringing out the papers in the form of book.

Bangalore

Dr. Rajasekhar
R. R. Biradar

Contents

Notes on Contributors

R.R. Biradar is a Lecturer, Department of Economics, Karnatak University, Dharwad.

Christu Das is the project co-ordinator of Dale View, a NGO working in Thiruvananthapuram district in Kerala state.

G. Dasarath Reddy is the Director of Action for Community Service Society, a NGO working with agricultural labourers, marginal farmers and women of backward communities in Chitoor District of Andhra Pradesh.

K. Joji is the Director of Social Action for Needy People, a registered NGO working in the field of empowerment, promoting leadership qualities and abolition of bonded labour in Doma Mandal of Ranga Reddy district in Andhra Pradesh.

K. Murugesan is the project head of Self-Help Association for Rural Education and Employment (SHARE)—a grass roots level organisation working for women's empowerment in Vellore district in Tamil Nadu.

N. L. Narasimha Reddy is an anthropologist and Director of 'Homo Sapiens'—a voluntary organisation working among the tribals in parts of Andhra Pradesh, primarily utilising government and local resources for their development and empowerment. Currently, he is also working for Andhra Pradesh Rural Livelihoods Project supported by DFID.

Mohd. Nooruddin is working for MARI, a NGO working in Warangal district of Andhra Pradesh. His areas of interest are Joint Forest Management, Community Development and Empowerment of the people.

Patrick Krause is associated with German Development Cooperation, Germany, and has been working on the institutional framework conducive for collaboration between different organisations.

P. Pushpa Rani is currently the Director of Ashraya, a non-profit organisation working for the cause of education for dropped out children in some parts of Hyderabad.

D. Rajasekhar is an Associate Professor (Economics), Decentralisation and Development Unit, in the Institute for Social and Economic Change, Bangalore.

M. V. N. Rao is the Director of Grama Vikas, a NGO working in the field of women's empowerment and mobilisation of the resources from the govenment in Kolar district in Karnataka.

N. Samson is working for GRAMA, a NGO working for rural development in Nizamabad and Adilabad districts of Andhra Pradesh.

T. Selwyn is working for the Centre for Rural Technology, a NGO working in the field of technological dissemination environment and micro-finance programmes in Nagercoil district in Kerala.

K. Sivaji is the Director of Sanghamitra Service Society, a NGO working in Krishna district in Andhra Pradesh.

P. Shobana is an ICSSR Doctoral Fellow, who previously worked in the Institute for Social and Economic Change, Bangalore.

D. M. Sridhar is the trustee of GRAMA, a NGO involved in the empowerment of rural women in several districts in Karnataka.

J. Srinivasa Rao is the Director of Chaitanya Jyothi Welfare Society, a registered NGO working for the empowerment of women in Nellore district of Andhra Pradesh.

Glossary

ACTS	Action for Community Service Society
APFD	Andhra Pradesh Forest Department
BCs	Backward Castes
CAPART	Council for People's Action for Rural Technology
CBOs	Community Based Organisations
CJWS	Chaitanya Jyothi Welfare Society
CMGs	Credit Management Groups
CRT	Centre for Rural Technology
DPAP	Drought Prone Area Programme
DRDA	District Rural Development Agency
DWCRA	Development of Women and Children in Rural Areas
GRAMA	Gramina Abhivrudhi Matthu Adhyayana Kendra
GTZ/SHF	German Development Cooperation/Self-Help Fund
IRDP	Integrated Rural Development Programme
ISEC	Institute for Social and Economic Change
JFM	Joint Forest Management
JRY	Jawahar Rojgar Yojana
MADA	Modified Area Development Agency
MHRD	Ministry of Human Resource Development
NABARD	National Bank for Agriculture and Rural Development
NCLP	National Child Labour Project
NFE	Non Formal Education
NGO	Non-Governmental Organisation
NOVIB	Netherlands International Cooperation for Development
OAP	Old Age Pension

PDS	Public Distribution System
PHC	Primary Health Centre
PMRY	Prime Minister Rojgar Yojana
PRIs	Panchayat Raj Institutions
RMK	Rashtriya Mahila Kosh
RRBs	Regional Rural Banks
SAGs	Social Action Groups
SANP	Social Action for Needy People
SCs	Scheduled Castes
SHARE	Self-Help Association for Rural Education and Employment
SHGs	Self-Help Groups
SIDBI	Small Scale Industrial Development Bank of India
STs	Scheduled Tribes
TRYSEM	Training of Rural Youths for Self-Employment
VSS	Vana Samrakshana Samithi
WASAN	Water and Sanitation Awareness Campaign

Introduction

D. RAJASEKHAR & R.R. BIRADAR

Since the inception of planning in India, the Government has launched several multi-faceted development strategies and programmes through various line departments to alleviate poverty. Even after five decades of state-led development efforts and interface with the community, rural India is still characterised by higher concentration of the poor, unemployment, hunger, malnutrition, starvation, illiteracy and gender inequality. It is being realised that the strategies of development ranging from individual to community development have failed to take the benefits of development to the poorest, and also to contain vested interests who not only oppress and exploit the poor but also appropriate the maximum benefits of the government managed development programmes. It is often felt that the agricultural and rural development programmes characterise goal confusion, mis-targetting and negative subsidies. The problem of leakage, pre-empting the benefits meant for the poor by the non-poor, is another major hurdle. The larger masses, weak and poor sections of the society are, therefore, subjected to only theoretical empowerment.

An important contributing factor for this state of affairs is that public institutions, established with a clear objective of giving support to the poor, have not been reaching them as there is no congruence between the recipient system and the delivery system. This is because of the failure to mobilise the poor to demand service and to obtain help from the government, which has resulted in very little interaction with the beneficiaries, and failure of the delivery system. In the absence of effective organisations, the poor have not been able to obtain their due share from these programmes. There is, therefore, need for an effective micro-level institutional arrangement in rural areas to involve the people in development programmes. Now, the general acceptance is that NGOs (Non-Governmental Organisations) provide an effective micro-level institutional arrangement in rural areas.

NGOs are believed to be efficient in introducing and sustaining micro-level institutions in countries where such institutions are needed and which had not existed before. NGOs, by virtue of being small in size, flexible, innovative and participatory can be more effective in their methods of organising the people, and in facilitating people's participation in development programmes aimed at ameliorating the socio-economic status of the poor (Wils 1996; Rajasekhar 1998). Despite NGO weaknesses such as spatial limitation, allegation on their accountability and constraints in working at micro levels, they have been gaining importance in service delivery and have become a prominent part of civil society. This has resulted in the proliferation of NGOs, diversification and multiplication of their activities and rapid flow of resources from government and donors (GOI 1992).

Based on a review of the development experience in many developing countries, scholars, most donors and some governments visualise that the sustained development process can be brought about through an improved relationship among the important development actors, namely, government, local self-government, NGOs and people's institutions (Edwards and Hulme 1992; Rajasekhar 1998). This is especially so in the case of interface between the government at various levels and NGOs (Sen 1999) for the simple reason that the government has sufficient resources but has failed in the efficient utilisation of the same due to lack of people's participation, innovative models, cost-effective strategies and so on. In the literature, the relationship between government and NGOs has received considerable attention because NGOs are believed to have these advantages. The groups of the poor, the formation of which has been facilitated by the NGOs, can now be effective as associations demanding services from the government and putting pressure on non-performing local development institutions.

From the mid-1980s, the number of government programmes implemented through NGOs and the quantum of state assistance channelled to them has significantly increased[1] (GOI 1985, 1992). The Seventh Five-Year Plan identified eighteen anti-poverty and minimum needs programmes where NGOs could be involved. The Eighth Five-Year Plan also defined the role of NGOs in improving the social delivery system and people's participation in the effective micro-level planning and development.

With the introduction of economic reforms in 1991, there has been a drive towards reducing the role of government in service delivery leading to a search for establishing a 'shadow state'. A 'shadow state' refers to a parastatal apparatus consisting of NGOs charged with the responsibility of providing services that would have otherwise been provided by the state (Wolch 1990). As a consequence, the NGOs are expected to enter into contractual agreements with the governments to play service delivery role as governments withdraw from such a role (Sen 1999). NGOs, which render such services, can broadly by termed as Public Service Contractors[2] (Korten 1990).

The recent years have witnessed an improved interface between government and NGOs in the areas of rural development and poverty alleviation. Various ministries and departments in the Central governments formulated schemes and programmes through which NGOs could access resources to plan, initiate and implement development activities for the poor in rural areas (Reddy and Rajasekhar 1996). At the local (i.e., state, district, and village) levels various programmes have been initiated by the government for the overall development of the poor and the marginalised. In the planning and implementation of these programmes, a role is foreseen for NGOs and space is provided to them to enable the poor to access resources (Rajasekhar and Reddy 1997). A role is also foreseen for them in influencing the government policies through lobbying and advocacy.

Notwithstanding these developments, the government and NGOs have been considered as 'reluctant partners' (Farrington *et al.* 1993). Others have perceived the interface between the government and NGOs as 'love-hate' and/or 'cat and mouse' relationship (PRADAN 1996). Some others perceive the relationship as "sweet and sour—sometimes sweet, sometimes sour and sometimes both sweet and sour" (PRIA 1989).

As India completes a decade of economic reforms and search for a 'shadow state', there is need to take stock of the interface between the government and NGOs. Can we still characterise the government and NGOs as 'reluctant partners'? Or, are they coming together? What are the factors contributing to the interface between government and NGOs? What strategies have been adopted to establish the interface, and what problems have been faced in this regard? At a broader level, there are questions on the very nature of interface between the government and NGOs. Whether the NGO sector should permanently supplement the development efforts of the government, and thereby, reduce the role of government? Or, whether the NGO sector should supplant the development efforts of the government, and thereby, make the government wither away from the development process? Or, whether NGOs should build-up the institutional capacity of the people to ensure responsiveness on the part of line departments, and influence the policies of the state in favour of the poor?

The Workshops

To address these questions, two workshops were organised on "Reluctant Partners Coming Together? Interface Between Government, NGOs and the People" in January and August 1999, at Hyderabad and Bangalore, respectively. The Hyderabad workshop was organised for the participants from Andhra Pradesh. Bangalore workshop was organised at the Institute for Social and Economic Change for the participants from Karnataka, Kerala and Tamil Nadu. These workshops were jointly organised by GTZ/SHF, Bangalore, Inter-cooperation (SDC), Hyderabad, Development Support Initiative (NOVIB) and ISEC, Bangalore. The participants in both the workshops included government officials, representatives of donor agencies, NGOs and academics. The chapters in this volume were presented at these two workshops, and were subsequently revised in the light of comments and suggestions from the workshop participants and the referees.

About the Volume

This volume includes 14 chapters. Chapter 1 analyses the type of interface between Government, NGOs and people, based on evidence, from nine NGOs from south India. Chapter 2 seeks to analyse the potential and problems in establishing institutional framework in which all the development actors including government and NGOs can collaborate and contribute for poverty alleviation.

Chapters 3 to 14 are contributions by NGOs in collaboration with the staff from ISEC, Bangalore. Seven papers have been contributed by NGOs from Andhra Pradesh. While two each have been contributed by NGOs from Karnataka and Tamil Nadu, one is based on the experience of one NGO from Kerala.

The structure of the Chapters 3 to 14 is more or less similar. Each of these NGOs presents the basic details on the organisation covering objectives, activities, number of villages covered, and the number of groups formed. The next aspect taken up for discussion is factors contributing to the interface with the government. Subsequently, these chapters discuss the strategies adopted in establishing interface, problems that NGOs and people encountered in the process. Most of these chapters also present the perception of the target group members on the quality of interface with the help of primary data collected by the ISEC staff. A structured questionnaire was canvassed among 20 sample members from three groups randomly selected for the purpose from each project area of NGOs. The questionnaire sought to collect information on the socio-economic background of the sample members of Self-Help Groups (SHGs), level of awareness, access and utilisation of government programmes, problems faced in approaching the officials and level of independence in accessing and utilising the government programmes.

The chapters put together form an interesting collection on issues, strategies and ways forward in so far as interface is concerned. The ensuing paragraphs summarise the main themes emerging from 14 chapters in this volume.

Reluctant partners?

As noted earlier, the government and NGOs are considered to be reluctant partners and the relationship between them is characterised as antoganistic. It is, however, not difficult to analyse the contributing factors for this characterisation. First, there are differences between government officials and NGOs on the very concept of poverty and this has been well brought out by Patrick Krause (Chapter 2 in this volume). The government officials perceive poverty to be the inability to access basic needs due to low income. In contrast, the NGOs have wider perception of poverty, which includes vulnerability; powerlessness, isolation and assetlessness.

There are also differences in their approaches to alleviate poverty. NGOs emphasise on the building of the organisations of the poor through process-oriented approach and strengthen their institutional capacity to address the root causes of poverty. The government officials, on the one hand, have doubts on this type of approach (Chapter 2), and on the other, like to adopt target-oriented approach to form a large number of groups in short space of time to quickly scale-up the activities and also for visible impact. This approach is often criticised by the NGOs, and hence there is reluctance to partner with the government. The government wants the relationship with NGOs to take place within the existing framework of bureaucratic procedures, formalities and accountability. As against this, the NGOs want the interface to take place in an atmosphere of partnership where there is flexibility in the programme.

As a result, different perceptions exist with regard to planning, implementation and monitoring of the programmes and also the very basis on which the programme has to be evaluated in terms of the utilisation of funds. The different perceptions give rise to doubts and lack of trust among government officials on accountability and transparency of NGOs. has lead to reluctant partnership. Hence, it has been noted that for government officials, the NGOs do not have the legitimacy and they are a front for foreign hands (PRADAN 1996).

It is not that there has been reluctant partnership between the government and NGOs in the case of all types of NGOs and during the entire post-independence period (Chapter 1 in this volume). The partnership between NGOs working with charity, welfare and development approach and government was often found as both the actors had shared objectives and beliefs on development. In contrast, the Social Action Groups and empowerment NGOs, which emerged in response to the failure of the government development models to contain poverty and oppression against certain sections, vehemently opposed the government development models and any relationship with the government other than critical collaboration.

Sen (1999) concludes that four types of relationship existed during the post-independence period : an era of co-operative relationship during the period of 1947 to late 1950s; an era of antagonistic relationship due to the emergence of social action groups and empowerment NGOs during the period 1960 to 1970s; an era of divergent relationship and state control during the period 1980s to early 1990s: and, the search for a shadow state during late 1990s (See, also, Chapter 1 in this volume). Therefore, it is difficult to accept the view that there was reluctant relationship between the government and NGOs during the entire post-independence period.

At this juncture it is necessary to mention that there is no truth in the general opinion that all government departments and officials and NGOs distrusted each other. Some of the departments actively collaborated with the NGOs. Some brureaucrats believed that the NGOs were the "eyes and ears" of the government (PRADAN 1996). Similarly, Gandhian charity and development NGOs actively collaborated with the government to reach the services to the people with whom they were working.

Chapters 3 to 14 provide considerable evidence that there is interface between government and NGOs. The data on source-wise distribution of total funding of the NGOs at two points in time (1996 and 1998) show that the share of government in the total development budget of NGOs increased during this period. A large number of NGOs accessed schemes and programmes initiated by the Central government. Even a larger number of them succeeded in enabling the poor to access resources from the government at the local level. In fact, quite a few of them, depended almost solely on government resources for both programme implementation and for generating costs towards salaries, training programmes, group formation, etc.

This evidence suggests that the governments and NGOs are no longer reluctant partners. Each of the actors has realised the advantages of the other and weakness of its own. The guidelines of the government programmes implemented in these areas stipulate that NGO participation is mandatory. Several NGOs mobilised resources from the government for the target groups. The number of target group members obtaining assistance and the total quantum of grant and loan availed from the government showed a significant increase in the late 1990s. The primary data show that the people benefited from the resources of the government and most of them reported an increase in employment and income. This shows that the government and NGOs are coming together to ensure that development inputs benefit the people.

What is an interface?

Interface implies the type of relationship between two organisations having similar objectives, activities and serving the same group of people. A review of the existing literature on types of interface has been made in Chapter 1. The available literature notes that there are three types of relationship between the government and NGOs, i.e., contractual collaboration, institutional collaboration and facilitated interface. It is argued in Chapter 1 that this typology does not include the role of donors in determining the type of interface and that factors contributing to interface are substantially different now as compared to the past. Based on what the dominant contributing factor is the interface may take three routes, namely, co-option, collaboration and critical collaboration.

Why interface is needed?

Chapters 3 to 14, which provide the factors contributing to the interface, suggest that four types of factors are important contributing factors. First set of factors is the type of objectives and activities with which each NGO begins. Objectives like empowerment of the target group makes it mandatory to organise the disadvantaged groups of women and men, build their confidence and strengthen their institutional capacity by providing training, awareness and leadership qualities to establish linkages with the government at various levels.

Second, NGOs consider interface with the government as essential to 'scale up' their development programmes. 'Scaling up' includes four components: organisational expansion, federation of people's institutions, working with the government to enable the target group to access the resources, and changing the government policies through lobbying and advocacy. With the realisation that they have spatial limitation and that the government controls the wide frameworks and policy environment within which people and their institutions have to operate, NGOs have begun to collaborate with the government not only to access the resources but also to influence the policies in favour of the poor.

Third, growth in the size of the target group and the need to meet their expectations compel the NGO to establish interface. With uncertain donor environment and realisation that they need to become autonomous and self-reliant, some of the NGOs, which initially depended almost entirely on external donor agencies for funding, have been experiencing the problems of reduced donor funds, and hence, have started looking for alternatives in terms of linkages. In some of the cases, donor agencies have also suggested that NGOs need to intervene to ensure that government resources reach the poor. All these factors have made NGOs, especially small ones, to establish linkages and mobilise the resources from the government.

Fourth, inability and lack of skills among the government officials to identify the poor and play a facilitating role to involve them in development process to address their basic needs motivate some of the NGOs to establish linkages.

What is the important contributing factor? It is concluded in Chapter 1 that uncertain donor environment is an important reason for establishing the interface. This implies that the nature of interface is most likely to have been either collaboration or co-option. What implication does this have on quality and susceptibility of interface is an outstanding issue.

What was the strategy adopted?

Chapters 3 to 14 discuss the strategies adopted by each NGO to establish linkages with the government. These strategies can be categorised under four types.

- The institutional capacity of the target group was sought to be enhanced by three ways to facilitate linkage with government at village and higher levels.
  - First, the target groups members were organised into SHGs to access the resources at the local level.
  - Second, the participation of the target groups in gram panchayats (both as voters and elected officials) was encouraged in some cases as it was felt that linkages with gram panchayats were important to access resources.

  - Third, participation in the NGO networks at district, state and national levels was considered to be important to influence the government policies in favour of the poor through lobbying and advocacy.
- Making the presence felt at the local level and building good-will among government officials was the next important strategy. Conducting workshops to familiarise the programmes to officials and organising face-to-face dialogue meetings between the people and officials on the need and problem of interface were two important methods used in this regard. Good-will was also sought to be built by attending all the meetings organised by the government departments.
- Striving for innovation in programme planning and implementation with an eye on establishing interface was yet another strategy.
- Whenever the applications, requests and letters did not yield significant results in establishing interface, the strategy of building pressure through processions, *dharnas* and visiting the offices in large numbers was adopted.

What was the main strategy adopted and why? The institutional strength was not utilised to its potential. The linkages between SHGs and gram panchayats were not substantive and meaningful. The evidence on networks having positive impact on interface (both in accessing resources and influencing policies and programmes of the government) was scanty. Similarly, the strategy of building pressure was not extensively used due to the fear that this might be politicised, and ultimately affect the good-will of officials towards NGOs. The strategy of making the presence felt was utilised by several NGOs with varying degrees of success. This discussion raises the following questions. Why is that NGOs do not utilise the institutional strength of the people to its potential? What contributes to the success and failure of each one of these strategies? Why is that NGOs are afraid to use the strategy of building the pressure? This volume provides answers to these questions.

What problems were encountered?

Establishing interface between the government and people was not an easy exercise for many NGOs. The important problems faced by the NGOs and/or target groups were: first, inordinate *delay in releasing the funds* which resulted in slow progress and even stoppage of development projects initiated by the NGOs. Second, while accessing the resources, a large number of NGOs faced the problems of *widespread corruption, confusing and complicating procedures,* non-availability of information and involvement of vested interests. Third, the *frequent transfer and discontinuity* of government officials made interface an extremely difficult and tortuous process. Fourth, frequent visits, appeasement or even bribing the bureaucrats who handled the government's developmental programmes were needed to ensure the speedy process relating to the movements of files, sanctioning of funds, providing of technical details of the schemes and so on. Fifth, low level of capacity and lack of motivation among lower level officials often became obstacles to the interface and this reportedly took a lot of time and energy of NGOs to convince and establish rapport with the government officials every time. Sixth, *widespread literacy* among target group members was a handicap to NGOs in providing awareness on various government departments, schemes, eligibility, procedure and so on.

The problems such as delays in releasing funds, complicated procedures, red tapism and corruption suggest that the co-option is the emerging type of interface. Problems such as illiteracy, ignorance and lack of information are more related to the critical collaboration; but, only a few of the NGOs seem to have faced these problems. The fact that the first type of problems is dominant suggests that there is reluctance between NGOs and the Government.

How did people perceive interface?

People perceived interface with the government to be important, and state that they were provided awareness on the programmes. However, there were variations in the level of awareness, access and utilisation of the programmes among the NGOs. There were also variations in terms of people actually visiting and interacting with the officials on their own. It is learnt that the target group members did not have to make repeated visits to the concerned office because the NGO itself mobilised the resources with the help of its influence and follow-up.

Evidence on levels of awareness, access and utilisation became meaningful if this was organised according the types of interface practised by nine NGOs (Chapter 1). Four NGOs were characterised by co-option, three of them pursue collaboration and two of them critical collaboration. An important finding has been that the level of awareness on government programmes was, in general, high among the target group members from the project areas pursuing critical collaboration. Same was the case with the levels of access (to a less extent) and utilisation. This suggests that the quality of interface was better in the case of NGOs characterised by critical collaboration since the people were on the forefront. There was also difference in so far as the dependence of the target group on NGOs was concerned. The people from the project areas of NGOs characterised by co-option depended somewhat heavily on NGOs, while those from the project areas of NGOs pursuing critical collaboration were far more independent.

What was the type of interface?

The perceptions of the people together with the evidence on the need, strategies and problems faced in the interface process suggests that co-option and simple collaboration were the dominant type of interface. In the case of NGOs characterised by co-option, the donor uncertainty together with the growth of the target group compelled them to have interface. The strategy of institutional strength was rarely used expect when there was delay in the sanctioning of the programme, delay in the release in the funds. The compulsion to obtain the resources at any cost forced them to get co-opted into the government framework of functioning. They hardly built the capacity of the people in accessing the resources on their own. Consciously or unconsciously, they developed dependence among the target group on NGOs. In the case of those pursuing the collaboration, the contributing factor was the same as that of the first type of NGOs. But, they were not able to pursue critical collaboration because this took enormous time and they might not have adequate funding support. They vehemently maintained that they might not have adequate funding support. They vehemently maintained that they were against getting co-opted by the government but did nothing to translate the principles of critical collaboration into practice.

In the case of NGOs pursuing critical collaboration, the objectives of the organisation were important contributing factors in influencing the decision for an interface. The strategy of institutional strength was used to enable the target groups to directly approach and access the resources. Facilitating and/or accompanying role, in terms of conducting dialogue meetings between the government officials and people, and building their capacity in approaching, accessing and utilising the resources, was played by these NGOs. These NGOs did face the problem of corruption, delays in the sanction of programmes and release of funds. But, by assigning a dominant role to the people in the interface process, these problems were countered to a large extent. Because of the above, the quality of critical collaboration interface was not only different but also had the potential to become sustainable.

The fact that co-option and collaboration were the dominant forms of interface suggests that the government is willing to collaborate with this type of NGO. The government does not seem to be willing to have institutional interface (Chapter 2). This implies that the funds will be made available only to those NGOs, which supplement and complement the government in service delivery. It appears that the government does not want to have critical collaboration with the NGOs.

This suggests that there is no substantive change in the quality of partnership. The government and NGOs are still "reluctant partners". If the NGOs are willing to get co-opted or supplement the government in service delivery through collaboration, the government does not have reluctance to partner with the NGOs. But, this is not acceptable to the NGOs. Even those NGOs characterised by co-option like to have only critical collaboration. But, they are compelled into this role. NGOs do not have any reluctance to partner with the government, if the interface is critical collaboration. But, the government is not willing to have such relationship.

If the government and NGOs are still reluctant partners, how does one explain the flow of resources to the NGOs and their target group? This does not look very paradoxical if one looks at the main problems faced by the NGOs and target group. Delays in the sanction of programme, complicated procedures, delays in the release of funds and corruption are the main problems faced, and this implies lack of trust among government officials on the accountability and transparency of NGOs. This, further, suggests that organisational features of one actor are not understood and appreciated by the other. The net result seems to be reluctance to partner with the other in true spirit for ensuring development benefits for the needy.

NOTES

1. The Seventh Five-Year Plan identifies eighteen anti-poverty and minimum needs programmes where NGOs can be involved. The Eighth Five-Year Plan also defines the role for NGOs in improving the social service delivery system and people's participation in effective micro-level planning. The government resources are being made available for NGOs working in the fields of safe drinking water, prevention of deforestation, social and economic development of children and women, primary health care, adult education and literacy, rural housing, bonded labour rehabilitation, etc.
2. These obtain projects/programmes from government or donors either by competitive tendering or through subcontracting on a non-competitive basis (Robinson 1997). These organisations provide services to the donors and governments in implementing development programmes, and are often driven by market factors rather than the values and motives that are generally associated with the NGOs.

REFERENCES

Edwards, Micheal and David Hulme (eds.) (1992). *Making a Difference : NGOs and Development in a Changing World.* London : Earthscan.

Farrington, John and Anthony Bebbington with Kate Wellard and David J. Lewis (1993). *Reluctant Partners? Non-Governmental Organisation, the State and Sustainable Agricultural Development.* London & New York : Routledge.

Government of India (GOI) (1985). *Seventh Five Year Plan, 1985-90.* Volume II : *Sectorial Programmes of Development.* New Delhi : Planning Commission.

Government of India (GOI) (1992). *Eighth Five Year Plan, 1992-97.* Volume I : *Objectives, Perspectives, Macro-Dimensions, Policy Framework and Resources* and Volume II; *Sectorial Programmes of Development.* New Delhi : Planning Commission.

Korten, D.C. (1990). *Getting to the Twenty-First Century : Voluntary Action and the Global Agenda.* West Hartford, CT: Kumarian Press.

PRADAN (1996). *Towards a Relationship of Significance : Interim Report on the Study of Relationships between Government and NGOs in Rajasthan.* New Delhi : Professional Assistance for Development Action.

PRIA (1989). *NGO-Government Relations : A Source of Life or a Kiss of Death?* New Delhi : Society for Participatory Research in Asia.

Rajasekhar, D. (1998). Rural Development Strategies of *NGOs. Journal of Social and Economic Development,* 1 (2) : 306-27.

Rajasekhar, D. and Narasimha Reddy (1997). *Local Development Programmes and NGOs : A Guide on Local and State Government Programmes for Fieldworkers.* Bangalore: BCO and NOVIB.

Reddy, N. L. Narasimha and D. Rajasekhar (1996). *Development Programmes and NGOs : A Guide on Central Government Programmes for NGOs in India.* Bangalore : BCO and NOVIB.

Robinson, M. (1997). Privatising the Voluntary Sector : NGOs as Public Service Contractors. In D. Hulme and M. Edwards (eds.), *NGOs, State and Donors : Too Close for Comfort.* New York : St. Martin's Press, Inc.

Sen, Sidhartha (1999). Some Aspects of State NGO Relationships in India in the Post-Independence Era. *Development and Change* , 30(2) : 327-55.

Wils, Frits (1996). Scaling up, Ministering and Accountability : The Challenge for NGOs. In Michael Edwards and David Hulme (eds.), *Non-Governmental Organisations—Performance and Accountability.* London : Earthscan.

Wolch, J.R. (1990). *The Shadow State : Government and the Voluntary Sector in Transition.* New York : The Foundation Centre.

1

People, Government and the NGOs

D. RAJASEKHAR & R.R. BIRADAR

INTRODUCTION

The importance of interface between the government and NGOs has been discussed in the introduction to this volume. While government, donor agencies and NGOs recognise the importance of interface, there is disagreement on the type of interface, and the role of people. In the literature, the interface has been characterised as "cat and mouse" and "sweet and sour". A book called the Government and NGOs as reluctant partners.

The decade of 1990s witnessed intensive discussion and debate on the type of interface. All the multi-lateral, bilateral and other donor agencies insist that the governments at various levels collaborate with NGOs in programme planing, implementation and monitoring. Several workshops, training programmes and consultations were held on how to bring about effective alliance between the government, NGOs and people. It is generally suggested that each of these actors should realise their comparative advantages and disadvantages, and work in such a way that effective development outcomes (equity, sustainability and efficiency) are brought about. Behind this suggestion, there is an assumption that the government and NGOs are still reluctant partners. In this context, the following questions arise. What is the nature of current interface? Are the government and NGOs still reluctant partners?

This chapter seeks to analyse the nature of interface between government, NGOs and the people on the basis of evidence from a large number of NGOs from south India. The main argument put forward is that the nature of interface is co-option and collaboration. The relationship between the government and NGOs is contractual and can be characterised as 'donor and recipient' relationship. The involvement of people is still marginal and the interface process is not progressing towards empowerment of the people.

INTERFACE BETWEEN GOVERNMENT AND NGOS IN INDIA

An analysis of interface between the government and NGOs cannot be introduced without delineating the typology of NGOs and the nature of interface established by each type of NGO with the government. Based on the objectives, ideologies, nature of activities and location, NGOs can be classified under four broad categories: operational or grass roots NGOs, support NGOs, network NGOs and funding NGOs. Their functions are:

Operational or Grass roots NGOs directly work with the oppressed sections of society. Some of them are big while others are small. The grass roots NGOs are either local based, working in a single and small project location, or working in multiple project areas in different districts, states and regions, covering a larger population. As the approach and orientation of grass roots NGOs also differ, the following distinction can be made among them. Charity and welfare NGOs are involved in charity (giving food, clothing, medicine, alms in cash and kind, etc.), welfare (providing facilities for education, health, drinking water, etc.), relief (responding to natural calamities like floods, drought, earthquakes and man-made calamities like refugee influx, ravages of war, etc.) and rehabilitation (undertaking the work in areas struck by calamities and starting activities durable in nature). Development NGOs are involved in providing (or facilitating the provision of) development services such as credit, seeds, fertilisers and technical know-how. Such NGOs concentrate on the development of the socio-economic environment of human beings.

Social Action Groups (SAGs) focus on mobilising marginalised sections around specific issues, which challenge the distribution of power and resources in a society. These NGOs are involved in raising the consciousness of the people, awakening, organising, recording of priorities to suit social justice, redeeming the past and opening the doors for opportunities to the oppressed and the exploited. Empowerment NGOs combine development activities with issue-based struggles. They may be involved in the provision of services such as savings and credit, but they utilise such activities for social, economic, political and cultural empowerment of the poor. The main difference between SAGs and empowerment NGOs is that the former do not normally undertake development activities as they believe in addressing the root causes of poverty. On the other hand, the empowerment NGOs undertake development activities because the people cannot undertake the struggles on 'empty stomachs'. They believe that empowerment of the people is an essential prerequisite for development. Hence, they strive hard to enable the people to become free from all the exploitative structures.

Support NGOs mainly provide services that would strengthen the capacities of grass roots NGOs, Panchayat Raj Institutions, Co-operatives and others to function more effectively through training programmes and by bringing out periodicals (Murthy and Rao 1997). Network NGOs are formal or informal associations of grass roots and/or support NGOs which meet periodically to act as a forum to share experiences, carry out joint development endeavours as well as engage in lobbying and advocacy. The participation of network NGOs in lobbying and advocacy is, however, a recent phenomenon. The primary activity of funding NGOs is to provide funding support to grass roots NGOs, support NGOs or people's organisations. Most of the funding NGOs in India obtain resources from foreign sources though efforts to raise funds from within India have, of late, assumed importance.

Interface between government and NGOs in the past

The interface between NGOs and the government in the past can be seen in four phases: co-operative relationship (1947 to late 1950s), antagonistic relationship (late 1960s to early 1970s), professional relationship (mid 1980s to early 1990s), and search for a shadow state (late 1990s).

Era of co-operation : 1947 to the late 1950s

Soon after independence, Gandhian and religious (both Christian and non-Christian) NGOs made their appearance in different parts of the country. The former were engaged in the promotion of agricultural and extension programmes, khadi and village industries, and livestock development. The latter were providing charity, relief and rehabilitation and also helping the poor to meet their health and nutrition needs, which should have been, otherwise, provided by the government. Government provided financial assistance and technical support to most of these NGOs (Chowdhary 1987; Maheshwari 1987) and engaged them in training the officials involved in the development process (Sen 1999; Kudva 1996). Many prominent people like late Jawaharlal Nehru opined that social work should be left to the NGO sector as it was capable of alleviating social problems while the government should extend financial and technical support (Chowdhary 1987).

These NGOs, which were welcomed by the government to become partners in its development process, remained as "silent partners" with the government. As the services delivered by such NGOs supplemented the government's effort, there was no conflict. Thus, a co-operative relationship developed as both the actors had common objectives and shared belief on development (Sen 1999; Kudva 1996).

Emergence of antagonism : the 1960s and 1970s

This phase witnessed the emergence of different types of NGOs: Development NGOs, Empowerment NGOs and SAGs[1]. Community Based Organisations (CBOs) were also formed by the poor themselves with or without NGO help. With a diversity in the institutional histories, motivation for forming these NGOs and their attitudes towards the government, the interface that emerged was also different.

Gandhian and religious NGOs continued to have the same functions (Sen 1999; Kudva 1996), though some of them expanded their activities to tackle the symptoms of poverty (low educational standards, ill-health, poor sanitation and housing) in a project mode, while others sought to enhance assets and income earning potential of the poor through activities relating to land development, credit, skills and extension services. A series of wars and droughts during this period contributed to a decline in funding to welfare and relief NGOs. It was speculated that this, in turn, contributed to the decline of charity and relief NGOs and general disillusionment with the government (Tandon and Brown 1990) leading to the emergence of antagonism.

The limited success of the government to overcome the problems of unemployment and poverty together with apathy of political parties and bureaucrats towards the poor contributed to the emergence of SAGs. Since the late 1970s, SAGs politicised the poor and poverty, and started to attack the dominant social and economic structure (Unia 1991; Sen 1999). The CBOs formed by them were antagonistic towards the government in their delivery system. The disillusionment with the government and its development models led to antagonism between the government and the SAGs. They were vociferous in their opposition to government programmes, which failed to improve the lives of the poor, weaker sections of the society and downtrodden (Ramachandran 1995).

The government extended its support to the welfare and development NGOs, but kept the SAGs at some distance as they were critical of the government policies. While the government supported foreign-funded welfare NGOs, it opposed and started to control the foreign funding for SAGs. The nature of interface between the government and SAGs was described as 'cat and mouse'. On the other hand, the development NGOs were looked upon favourably because they supplemented the government's development efforts. Thus, during this phase, while the welfare, Gandhian and development NGOs collaborated with the government, SAGs were critical of the government resulting in either antagonistic relationship or no collaboration.

Diversity of Government—NGO relationship: the 1980s & 1990s

This phase of Government-NGO collaboration saw the following three important trends. With the maturing of the NGO sector, young professionals, retired bureaucrats, members of political parties, and business people, motivated by job prospects rather than commitment to radical social transformation, started to work at the grass roots. Some of them provided support (research consultancy, training, evaluation and documentation) to the government, smaller NGOs and CBOs. As the NGO sector was undergoing diversification, the nature of interface also started to take different shape. NGOs seemed to have moved from a focus on relief and welfare (first generation) to address the structural context of local self-help action, formation of people's institutions and mobilising the local resources (second generation). This included seeking changes in the institutions and policies at national and sub-national levels that inhibited effective self-help action (third generation) (Korten 1987).

The institutional histories, the social origins and motivations of the NGOs became important in shaping the nature of interface. For instance, the NGOs, started by retired bureaucrats, established quick and good relationship with the government, and managed to obtain government funds for establishing NGOs and for undertaking development activities.[2] Similarly, in order to maintain good relationship with the government for pragmatic reasons such as their survival, support NGOs depended on the government projects.

Second, while the empowerment NGOs started to collaborate with the government as the concerns for survival dominated, the SAGs began to include development component in their projects as they realised the difficulties in sustaining struggle-oriented activities without meeting the basic needs of the target group. Thus, by mid-1980s some SAGs began to collaborate with the government in order to include development component in their projects. However, this was not a general phenomenon. Some SAGs continued to have antipathy towards government, saw the government as oppressive and exploitative, and opposed the government policies on the grounds that these would impoverish the poor further (Chandhoke and Ghosh 1995).

Third, this phase also witnessed the emergence of network NGOs to take up some strategic issues of government policies in relation to energy, environment, women's rights, anti-arrack movement, eradication of dowry and poverty by advocacy and lobbying. Such NGOs established mostly a critical collaboration with the government, for instance, the Narmada Bachao Andolon[3]. There have been initiatives aimed at establishing NGO networks at different levels (Rajasekhar and Nair 1995) with an explicit objective of influencing the government policies in favour of the poor though the concerns of fund raising and recognition also dominated the agenda.

To check the rapid growth in the NGO sector, the government sought to control their operations by defining their role and introducing stringent regulations[4]. This contributed to a further divide between the government, and empowerment NGOs and SAGs.

Moving towards an era of 'Shadow State'

Though the government made efforts to establish a 'Shadow State' soon after independence, it gained momentum only with the introduction of economic reform, prescriptions to reduce the government role in social sector development and a decline in the budget for the social sector. Over time, the government gradually transferred the responsibility of social services to the NGO to establish a 'Shadow State'[5]. The NGOs, therefore, were expected to assume greater role in providing social services. They were also expected to mobilise the poor and build up their institutional capabilities by forming organisations among them to enable them to reap the benefits of economic development arising out of globalisation. However, setting up a 'Shadow State' faced many deterrents such as delay in the disbursement of funds, red tapism and the apathy of bureaucrats (Sen 1999).

To conclude, immediately after independence, there was no conflict between the government and NGOs as they had common objectives and beliefs on development. Subsequently, the nature of government and the socio-political context under which the NGOs emerged shaped the nature of interface. In the late 1990s, the government started making efforts to establish a 'Shadow State' to transfer its role in service delivery. Thus, the nature of interface largely depended on organisational complexities, identities, motivations, its social origin and histories, characteristics and political, social and economic realities, local politics, the actions of local agents, local institutional behaviour with local government, views of individuals and nature of NGOs' own programmes (Sen 1999).

CONCEPT AND TYPES OF INTERFACE

In simple terms, interface implies type of relationship between two organisations having similar objectives, activities and serving the same group of people. In the literature, three types of relationship between government and NGOs (contractual collaboration, institutional collaboration and facilitative interface) have been discussed.

Contractual collaboration

The contractual arrangements may be bilateral or schematic. Bilateral relationship refers to a situation where a single NGO enters into an agreement with the government to perform certain pre-defined tasks, and hence, this can be termed as one-to-one relationship. The salient features of this are measurable outputs, fixed targets, pre-determined costs and, reimbursement of funds when tasks are complete. It is the government that can change the programme and evaluate with its own criteria. Once the NGOs enter into an agreement, they have little flexibility as the powers to modify programme norms rest with the government. Selection of NGOs or dropping them is done at the discretion of officials (Ramachandran 1995). But, flexibility to NGOs depends on what level the agreement has been entered into and the reimbursement of funds depends on the evaluation outcomes.

Contractual collaboration may also be schematic in which the government, in order to fulfil its targets, involves NGO participation in implementing its schemes. A large number of NGOs receive funds from the government under a common scheme, and hence, this can be termed as many-to-one relationship. With little flexibility to modify the schemes in accordance with the specific needs of the poor, the needs of the local people and their participation at different levels are rarely considered. The government does not approach the target group members directly. The relationship between the government and NGOs is of donor and recipient. There is no forum for NGOs to offer their feedback on the implementation of the programme or any innovative way of implementation (Figure 1.1).

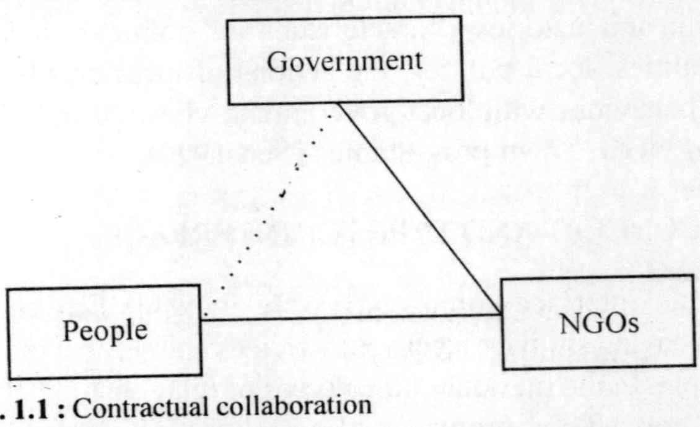

Fig. 1.1 : Contractual collaboration

Note: Thick line indicates direct interface and the dotted line indicates indirect interface.

Institutional interface

Under this arrangement, the government and the NGOs perform inter-related roles and work with each other for meeting shared development goals. The NGOs play a complementary role in the formation of groups, providing training and awareness, and ensuring equity and participation, while government implements physical works through the groups formed by the NGOs. In this form, since NGOs are assigned more of a process-oriented role, the targets to be achieved are both quantitative and qualitative.

Important features of institutional interface are relative flexibility enjoyed by the NGOs in their budgets and greater opportunity for mutual exposure and cross learning between the government and the NGOs (PRADAN 1996). The three way links—Government, NGOs and target-group—are strong. This implies that these three actors have direct relationship, and thus, utilise their comparative advantages towards evolving innovative methods of planning and implementation (Figure 1.2). The NGOs have to be more accountable and transparent in their actions and performance.

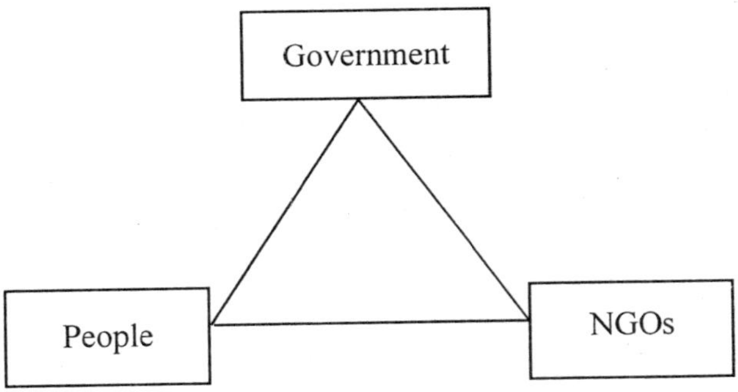

Fig. 1.2 : Institutional interface

Facilitative interface

In mutually facilitative interface the NGOs interact with the government machinery on a variety of issues concerning the communities with which they work, whether or not the government seeks their help on these issues. Both government and NGOs agree on the merit of these issues but their approaches and motivation may differ. The NGO will play an important role in capacity-building of the target group while seeking to strengthen the links between government and the target group. The NGO role with the government is catalytic—pro-actively supporting and inducing it to respond to the people's needs. The government has direct contact with the target group, while the role of NGO is that of facilitator (Figure 1.3). There is no direct financial relationship between the government and the NGO. The strong link between the government and the target-group is found at different levels of development process and is sustainable. Depending on the issues at hand, the required intervention, the strategy adopted by the NGOs and government's response, the nature of interface may change over time.

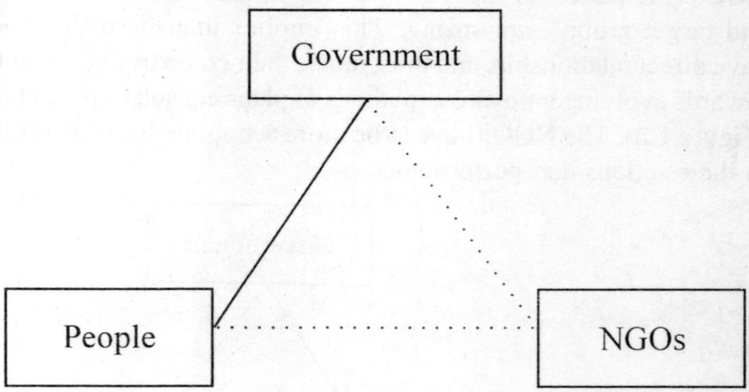

Fig. 1.3 : Facilitative interface

The above topologies do not include the role of donors. With the recent introduction of economic reforms to bring about the efficient use of resources and prescription that the role of government in service delivery should be reduced, there has been a search for establishing a more pronounced 'Shadow State'. In the light of economic liberalisation and structural adjustment programmes, most of the third world governments had to cut down their expenditure on public services in a phased manner and also gradually reduce their role in social and economic development of the country. In this context, NGOs are expected to enter into contractual agreements with donor or governments to play a service delivery role to provide public services as governments withdraw from such role (Sen 1999). NGOs, which render such services, can broadly be termed as Public Service Contractors[6] (Korten 1990).

Thus, the factors making it imperative for the interface are substantially different now as compared to the past. With the emergence of empowerment NGOs and change in strategies of SAGs, each of the organisations may have recognised the strength of the other and weaknesses of its own, and hence, is willing to collaborate. Second, there may be compelling factors (such as changes in donor policies) for both government and NGOs to collaborate with the other. Based on which of the above is a dominant factor, the interface may take three routes.

Mobilisation of government resources by NGOs for the poor

Here, the NGOs play a dominant role as compared to the people and government because they are compelled to mobilise the resources for their survival or the donor agency has prescribed such a role. This may be called as collaboration between the government and NGOs (Figure 1.4) wherein the latter participate in the mobilisation of schemes and programmes meant for their target group at the instance of donors.

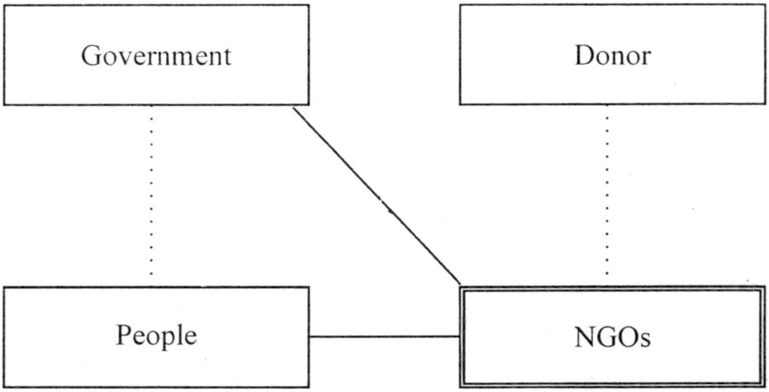

Fig. 1.4 : Collaboration

Implementation of government programmes or service delivery by NGOs for the poor

This may take the form of collaboration or co-optation of NGOs by the government. The former would take place when each organisation recognises (or made to recognise) the strengths of the other. Government by contracting out certain activities and services takes the assistance of NGOs, and co-opts them into the mode of government functioning. In this, the role of government is dominant as compared to the people and the NGOs. The collaboration takes place within the existing framework of government policies, approach and procedures, and there may not be much scope for either people or NGOs to change this framework (Figure 1.5).

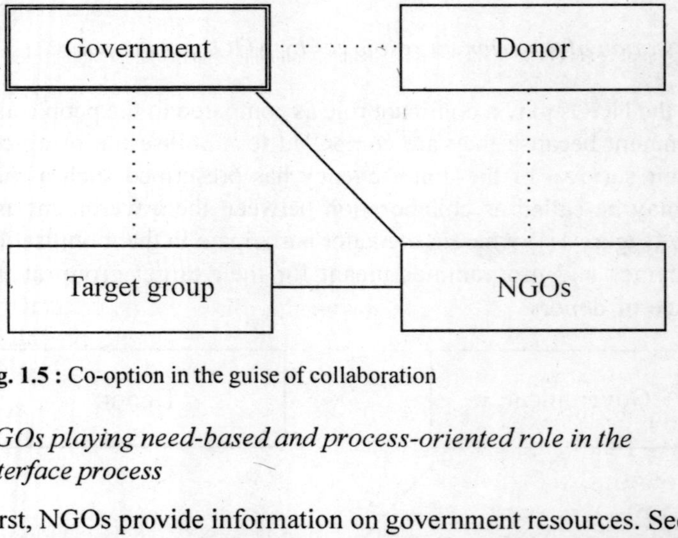

Fig. 1.5 : Co-option in the guise of collaboration

NGOs playing need-based and process-oriented role in the interface process

First, NGOs provide information on government resources. Second, they build the capacity of the people in accessing the resources within the framework of rights and entitlements and effectively utilising the same. Third, building organisational strength among the poor not only to question the parameters that determine the quantum and flow of resources to the poor (policy advocacy) but also to ensure regular flow of resources to the poor (sustainability). In the entire process, NGOs would play an active role in the beginning, and subsequently, people would play a dominant role as compared to the NGOs and the government (Figure 1.6). This process may be called critical collaboration wherein the NGOs and the people collaborate with the government, while at the same time criticise those government policies which are anti-poor (Reddy and Rajasekhar 1996).

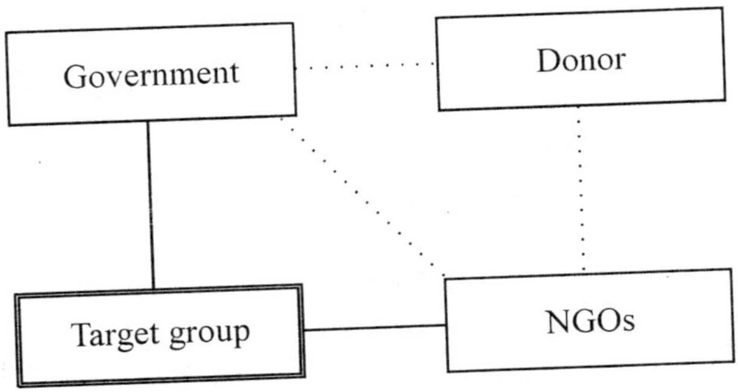

Fig. 1.6 : Critical Collaboration

INTERFACE BETWEEN GOVERNMENT, NGOs AND PEOPLE : EVIDENCE

The foregoing discussion suggests that there have been changes in the nature of interface during the post-independence period. What is the emerging and predominant type of interface? To answer this question, this chapter puts together the primary data collected from nine NGOs from South Indian states, the case studies on which are included in this volume. Four NGOs are from different districts in Andhra Pradesh, two are from Karnataka, one from Kerala and two from Tamil Nadu. These organisations emerged in different years; but the origin of most of them could be traced either to late 1980s or early 1990s.

Did these NGOs establish any interface with the government? An answer to this question can be found from the evidence on the proportion of government funds in the total budget of the NGO programmes, number of target group members availing assistance from the government and quantum of such assistance. The distribution of total budget by different sources in 1996 is compared with that in 1998 (Table 1.1). This information, which could not be obtained from all the NGOs for both the years, shows that the total quantum of funding has increased in almost all the NGOs. Between 1996 and

Table 1.1 : Details of funds mobilised by the NGOs

NGOs	*Total funding (Rs.)*	*Proportion of funding in 1996 by*			*Total funding (Rs.)*	*Proportion of funding in 1998 by*		
		Donor	*Self*	*Government*		*Donor*	*Self*	*Government*
NGO 1	—	—	—	—	4,150,026	18.73	44.82	36.46
NGO 2	1,351,500	22.20	—	77.80	866,000	20.55	—	79.45
NGO 3	1,465,653	82.67	—	17.67	2,875,748*	95.55	—	4.45
NGO 4	1,191,645	48.40	—	51.60	3,835,232	19.74	—	80.26
NGO 5	—	—	—	—	25,193,544	32.03	17.73	50.24
NGO 6	4,908,587	71.75	11.68	16.57	7,337,392	54.95	26.34	18.71
NGO 7	6,919,093	23.60	45.01	31.39	9,547,394	15.87	38.17	45.10
NGO 8	—	—	—	—	4,341,127	19.20	75.55	5.25
NGO 9	5,244,130	89.74	3.29	6.97	2,299,190	51.04	42.56	6.38
All NGOs	21,080,608	56.70	18.30	25.00	60,445,653	33.23	26.74	40.03

*Data pertain to 1997.

Source : Compiled from the case studies of NGOs.

1998, the share of donors in the total funding of all the NGOs declined, while that of government increased. In 1996, the share of donors in the total fund was relatively high in NGOs 9, 6 and 3. By 1998, the share of government was substantially high in NGOs 4, 2, 5 and 7. Interestingly, in the case of three NGOs (8, 1 and 9) own sources became significant. One of these NGOs runs a production-cum-marketing centre, and the resources are being utilised for development activities. Another NGO has its own income generation centre (started with the support of donor) and the proceeds of which are used for developmental activities. More importantly, only four NGOs (3, 6, 9 and 5) depended somewhat heavily on donors in 1998 for carrying out the development of the target group. This information, thus, indicates that there is a shift in the dependence of NGOs from donors to government.

Table 1.2 further corroborates this. There is substantial increase in the number of target group members and quantum of resources obtained from the government. The average amount of assistance also increased. However, there are differences across the states in so far as the increase in average amount of assistance is concerned. Although the number of target group members receiving government programmes increased at a rapid rate in the case of NGOs from Andhra Pradesh, the quantum of assistance increased at a slow rate. Consequently, the average amount of assistance declined. In the case of target group members from Karnataka and Kerala the average amount was not only high but also increased as much of the assistance was obtained as loan from banks and other agencies.

Table 1.2 : Mobilisation of resources from the government by NGOs

NGOs from	*No of people obtaining the resources*		*Amount of grant/loan (Rs)*		*Average amount of assistance (Rs)*	
	1996	1998	1996	1998	1996	1998
Andhra Pradesh	2,488	4,025	4,034,569	5,586,889	1,622	1,388
Karnataka	1,348	1,989	4,928,500	14,053,440	3,656	7,066
Kerala	357	471	4,646,668	8,187,962	13,016	17,384
Tamil Nadu	NA	NA	NA	NA	NA	NA
Total	4,193	6,485	13,609,737	27,828,291	3,246	4,291

NEED FOR INTERFACE

The above discussion suggests that most of the NGOs have established interface with the government. What has been the type of interface? The evidence on perceived need for interface by NGOs has been examined below to obtain some clues on the type of interface practised. For instance, if the empowerment of the poor is the main factor making it necessary to have interface, then critical collaboration is the likely outcome. When the concerns such as insufficient budget to pay salaries, etc., influence the NGOs to have interface, they may be forced to get co-opted by the government.

Objectives and activities

For a majority of the NGOs, empowerment of the target group is an important objective. In broader terms, empowerment is defined as "a process where powerless people become conscious of their situation and organise to empower and access opportunities: an outcome where poor women and men can take control over their lives, set their own agenda, skills, solve problems, develop self-reliance" (Mayoux and Johnson 1997). Four dimensions of empowerment can be distinguished: power within, individual changes in confidence and consciousness. Power to: increase in skills, abilities, including earning on income, access to markets and networks; power over : changes in power relations within the households, communities and at the macro level; and power with: organisation of the powerless to enhance individual abilities and/or ability to challenge and change power relations.

If the above is the conceptual background to empowerment, then the activities such as imparting education and awareness, and raising consciousness are needed to bring changes within. Organising training programmes, therefore, becomes an important activity, which has been undertaken by almost all the NGOs. Second, mobilising the target group into organisations, and sustain them through activities such as savings and credit and interface with the government is necessary to enable the target groups to have power within, power over, and power with. Five out of 9 NGOs stated that they organised the disadvantaged groups of women and men, built their confidence and strengthened their institutional capacity by providing training, awareness and leadership qualities to establish linkages with the government at various levels. The following efforts to make the government machinery quickly respond to the felt needs of the poor were also made. The confidence within the target group was sought to be built by providing information on government programmes, building their capacity to approach the government officials and access the resources meant for them. To facilitate the process, some of the organisations also conducted dialogue meetings with the concerned officials.

Scaling up and influencing the government policy in favour of the poor

The NGOs have spatial limitation (Webster 1995). Further, they are not 'magic bullets' (Edwards and Hulme 1995) to solve all problems of the poor. Interface with government development machinery is, therefore, considered to be essential for NGOs to 'scale up' their development programmes. Since the government controls the wide frameworks and policy environment within which people and their institutions have to operate, two of the NGOs stated that they sought to have a positive and creative relationship with the government agencies. This not only enables the poor to assert their rights and help them in getting benefits from the government but also provides grass roots experience to get integrated into micro-level planning.

These NGOs also stated that interface was needed to support innovative schemes of the government. If the government initiated pro-poor and people-centred development programmes, NGOs came forward to contribute their comparative advantages for the success of the programmes. Even if the government development paradigm was not favourable to the poor, at times NGOs entered into collaboration with the government to get a chance to change the policy climate or programme approaches. Establishing linkages has been felt necessary by three out of four NGOs to influence the government policies in favour of the poor. Though the NGOs were working in limited areas, they could change the perception of the government on planning, implementation, maintenance and evaluation of development interventions through lobbying, advocacy and networks so that the poor in those areas not covered by the NGOs could also be benefited in the process.

Growth in the size of the organisation

The growth in the size of the target group and the need to meet their expectations may have compelling impact on NGOs to establish interface process. The size of target group of all the NGOs increased between 1996 and 1998. Correspondingly, there has been an increase in the size of NGOs in terms of villages, people's institutions and target group members (Table 1.3).

Such an increase implies that the resources required to administer the projects, and also to meet the hopes and aspirations of the target group members had to be increased. However, the late 1990s also witnessed an uncertain donor environment in terms of declining foreign funds to Indian NGOs. The priorities and perceptions of external donor agencies operating within India also changed. Besides, the perception of many donor agencies regarding what factors contribute to poverty and what are poverty alleviating strategies seems to be changing. All these imply that there are dangers in NGOs developing dependence on external donors (Reddy and Rajasekhar 1996:9).

Table 1.3 : Changes in the number of villages, SHGs and total target group members

NGOs		*No of villages*		*No of SHGs formed*		*Target group members*	
		1996	*1998*	*1996*	*1998*	*1996*	*1998*
NGO	1	9	11	40	84	510	1,068
NGO	2	20	40	37	110	592	1,760
NGO	3	20	50	95	271	2,050	4,840
NGO	4	28	75	53	93	1,579	3,500
NGO	5	104	112	114	172	3,488	3,790
NGO	6	40	136	160	309	3,153	4,816
NGO	7	5	7	256	336	8,560	11,483
NGO	8	27	50	NA	9	NA	NA
NGO	9	25	30	25	30	750	750
All NGOs		278	511	780	1,414	20,682	32,007

In this context, establishing linkages and mobilising resources from different sources, especially from the government, have become necessary for the NGOs. To begin with, most of the NGOs were implementing their development programmes mainly with the funds obtained from external donor agencies. The quantum and direction of funds from donor agencies kept changing and thereby creating donor uncertain environment. Some of the NGOs have been experiencing the problems of uncertain donor environment in terms of reducing funds. Table 1.1 reveals that percentage share of funds mobilised from donor agencies by most of the NGOs moderately declined during 1996-98. This made many NGOs to establish linkages and mobilise resources from the government.

Of late, donor agencies have been suggesting that the resources at the disposal of central and state governments have not properly been used to alleviate poverty, and that NGOs need to facilitate the flow of these resources for poverty alleviation. For instance, one of the NGOs reported that the bilateral agencies had stipulated some conditions to participate in mobilising the resources available with the government. NGOs have also started realising the fact that continued dependence on foreign funding not only limits their autonomy but also does not sustain the development process. This has contributed to the establishment of improved interface with the government to enable the people to access the resources and to develop their demand systems.

Most of the small NGOs face the shortage of funds to meet the salaries of their permanent staff. Such a resource crunch often forces them to participate in any on-going government programmes to obtain resources, and thereby reduce the tension of seeking funds elsewhere. However, this problem is not acute among large NGOs as they have greater organisational capacity to mobilise funds from international donors. In view of the ever increasing needs of the poor and the activities of the NGOs, the development funds either in the form of group savings or donor agencies tends to become insufficient. To raise adequate resources to meet the fund requirements, establishing linkages and access the resources are of utmost importance to newly started and large NGOs. This has been found to be happening in the case of four NGOs.

Four of the NGOs stated that the government had vast resources. However, these resources were being cornered by the affluent sections of the society due to lack of institutional capacity of the poor to demand their due share from the system and the government. These influenced them to initiate the process of interface with the government.

Limited success of government programmes

Inability and lack of skill among the government officials to identify the poor and play a facilitating role to involve them in the development process to address their basic needs motivated six NGOs to establish linkages. Four NGOs noted that the government programmes failed to reach the poor. Two of the NGOs stated that many of the government officials were not even aware of some of the programmes started by their department. To provide information and publicise these programmes with the officials as well as people, establishing linkages was felt necessary by two NGOs to achieve better results.

To conclude, most of the NGOs stated that uncertain donor environment was an important reason for establishing the interface. On the basis of this, one can conclude that the nature of interface is most likely to have been either collaboration or co-option. But, some of these NGOs also stated that their own programme, objectives, and limited success of government programmes contributed to the interface. Thus, the evidence on need for interface is mixed. Let us, therefore, look at evidence on strategies.

STRATEGIES ADOPTED IN ESTABLISHING INTERFACE

Institutional building

One of the important strategies of the NGOs was the formation and promotion of SHGs. The NGOs, which combined empowerment and development component in their work, sought to build people's institutions based on self-help and establish linkages with government departments with a view to either tapping the resources or changing the state-led development paradigm by involving the government machinery in the process. Although the formation of people's institution was used as an entry point in the interface process by almost all the NGOs, only five of them explicitly mentioned that this strategy was adopted as an important means to establish linkages and access resources.

The participation of target group members in gram sabhas and as members in the gram panchayats has potential to influence the development agenda of local decentralised government in favour of the poor. Almost all the NGOs stated that they realised the importance of participation of target members in local decentralised government in making a difference in the quality of development at the local level. Some of them also enabled their target group members to contest and win the election. The discussions, however, reveal that while some of them have ideas on how participation of the target group in gram panchayats helped the interface, others did not have much idea. On the whole, the evidence is that there are no substantive and meaningful linkages between SHGs formed by the NGOs and local decentralised government.

While SHGs are necessary means to establish linkages with the local government, NGO networks at district, state and national levels are being increasingly used to establish interface with the government at higher levels[7], and influence their policies and programmes. In recent years, networking among NGOs has undergone a phenomenal growth. Many NGOs are the members of networks at district and state levels; but the evidence on networks having positive impact on interface (both in accessing the resources and influencing the policies and programmes of the government) is scanty.

Building goodwill among the government officials

The organisation of workshops and meetings with government officials contribute to the process of interface. By conducting workshops and conferences, NGOs can present their activities and progress to different development actors. Three NGOs stated that they organised workshops and meetings for which people's representatives and government officials were invited. The NGOs made presentation on their programmes including number of villages covered, number of groups formed and activities undertaken by them. While doing this, the NGOs used their comparative advantages. Maintenance and updating of records on development activities of NGOs helped in rendering prompt and quick responses to enquiring officials. This also showed that the NGOs were transparent. Secondly, impressive presentation of the problem of the poor with proper data and information also helped. This created positive appreciation among the development partners especially government, leading to interface process and people accessing the resources.

Holding face-to-face dialogue meetings between the poor and the government officials at mandal/block/taluk/district level has been used by some of the NGOs as an important strategy to present the felt needs of the community and work out ways and means to address them. At the dialogue meetings, the people could also put forward the problems faced in accessing the government programmes. This sort of dialogue meetings was being used as a means to establish improved interface between the government at various levels and the people at grass roots (Rajasekhar and Reddy 1997). For instance, seven NGOs conducted face-to-face dialogue meetings inviting people, elected representatives of gram panchayats, government officials to share grievances, felt needs and problems faced by the poor in accessing the resources.

The participation of NGO staff in the meetings or discussions organised by the government is also an important contributing factor in establishing and sustaining the interface process. Many NGOs reported regular participation of their staff at the government meetings, training programmes, review meetings, exposure, etc., and thereby building rapport with the government officials.

Five of the NGOs utilised demonstration and procession to build pressure on government officials. Whenever there was a delay in releasing the resources and non-response from the government officials, demonstration and procession, calling press meetings, organising *dharnas*, direct letter correspondence were the strategies used by these NGOs to put pressure on government officials.[8] The demonstration and procession by NGOs made the government officials more alert and showed their confidence in bringing changes in the prevailing institutional framework in favour of their clients.

Evolving suitable models

Innovative and cost-effective models of NGOs would attract the government development machinery towards them in jointly undertaking the development work. The same was the case with four NGOs, which developed innovative, and people-centred approach in the identification of the poor, formation and development of SHGs in micro-finance. Attracted by these approaches, banks established interface with SHGs under NABARD's programme. This has helped build up a strong relationship with banks and NABARD.[9]

To conclude, the discussion on strategies adopted by NGOs does not provide conclusive evidence on the type of interface because of the following. Most of the NGOs have not utilised the strength of the people's organisations to establish and sustain the process of interface. Although all of them have formed and promoted SHGs, the way in which the collective strength of the people in the groups was used to establish interface was not clear. This indicates that collaboration or co-option is the predominant type of interface. Although building pressure on government officials is cited by most of the NGOs as a strategy, this itself cannot be taken as evidence pointing towards critical collaboration. This is because dialogue meeting *per se* does not suggest any type of collaboration. What is important is the role and participation of people in these meetings. Further, dialogue meeting would become necessary even in collaboration and co-option type of interface. On the whole, based on the evidence on need and strategies, one cannot conclude the type of interface. Hence, the problems faced by the NGOs have been discussed below to ascertain the type of interface.

PROBLEMS FACED BY THE NGOS AND TARGET GROUP

Establishing interface between the government and people was not an easy exercise for many NGOs, whose hands were often into the pockets of the government. As a matter of fact, many bureaucrats did not welcome the entry of NGOs into the domains of government, as this threatened to reduce their importance in the eyes of the people. Therefore, the government officials were often a major hurdle in the process of establishing the interface. Some of the problems faced by either NGOs and/or target group members while establishing linkages and mobilising the resources have been discussed.

- One of the widespread and persistent problems was the inordinate *delay in releasing the funds* (PRADAN 1996; Sen 1999; Bhat and Satish 1993; AVARD 1992), which have resulted in slow progress and even stoppage of development projects initiated by the NGOs. This problem seems to be continuing. Almost all the NGOs reported that they faced the problem of inordinate delays in getting the funds released.

- While accessing the resources, a large number of NGOs faced the problems of *widespread corruption, confusing and complicating procedures,* non-availability of information and involvement of vested interests. There are innumerable rules and regulations to be fulfilled by the NGOs. This led to further delay in the completion of the project and deriving the results.
- It was mentioned that the NGOs promoted by the politicians and contractors did not hesitate to bribe the officials and had a tendency to keep information to themselves. Therefore, they were far more successful in mobilising the resources as compared to those NGOs with social commitment and values.
- Another serious problem has been the *frequent transfer and discontinuity* of government officials. An enormous amount of time and energy was spent to re-establish their credentials and familiarise and convince the new incumbents the need for fulfilling commitments made by his/her predecessor. This effort would be a waste if the new person was against the interface or did not honour the commitment made by the preceding officer.
- Frequent visits, appeasement or even bribing the bureaucrats who handle the government's developmental programmes are needed to ensure the speedy process relating to the movements of files, sanctioning of funds, providing of technical details of the schemes and so on. This needs to be seen in the context that most of the officials are not positive in their thinking and attitude towards NGOs, and there exists mutual distrust. This happened when NGOs were perceived to encroach upon the professional domain of government functionaries and gaining goodwill of the local people as against the government.
- Low level of capacity and lack of motivation among lower level officials often became obstacles to the interface and this reportedly took lot of time and energy of NGOs to convince and establish rapport with the government officials every time.

- Establishing linkages between the government officials and the target group become easy when the latter are literate and cognisant. *Widespread illiteracy* among target group members was a problem while facilitating the linkage process with the government. Due to illiteracy, the people were not very well aware of the various government departments, schemes, eligibility, procedure and so on.
- *Lack of dissemination of information* on rural development programmes designed by the government at higher levels to lower level officials was another problem. The decisions were orally communicated leading to confusion and lack of clarity. At times, this also led to manipulation by the lower level officials.
- *Local political intervention* in many of the internal affairs was cited by two NGOs to be another problem. The local political leaders driven by vested interests often caused hindrance in establishing linkages and access the resources to the poor since their importance in the eyes of the poor would decline.

This discussion also does not provide conclusive evidence on the type of interface though it suggests that co-option is the emerging type of interface. In the literature (PRADAN 1996; Bhat and Satish 1993; Sethna and Shah 1993; AVARD 1992), delays in releasing funds, complicated procedures, red tapism and corruption were cited to be important problems in establishing interface in early 1990s. Interestingly, these are the problems faced by almost all the NGOs in our study. This implies that all types of interface are possible, and that, interface is not institutionalised. Problems such as illiteracy, ignorance and lack of information are more related to the critical collaboration; but, only a few of the NGOs seem to have faced these problems. Hence, there is need to turn to people's perceptions on the interface to find out the type of interface.

PERCEPTIONS OF THE TARGET GROUP MEMBERS

Primary data from 176 members of SHGs in the project areas of nine NGOs were collected. The questionnaire canvassed among these members covered questions on socio-economic background, levels of awareness, access and utilisation of government programmes, problems faced in approaching the officials and levels of independence in approaching and accessing the programmes.

In each NGO project area, data were collected from 20 members randomly selected from three groups in three villages. The distribution of 176 members by land ownership shows that about one-third each were landless and marginal farmers. Less than one-fourth were small farmers. Thus, over 90 per cent of the sample were landless, marginal and small farmers. The caste background of members shows that nearly 45 per cent of them belonged to SC/ST categories, while about 37 per cent belonged to backward castes. This information shows that most of the members were poor and belonged to the depressed castes.

The sample members stated that they were provided with information on various schemes of the government. The methodology of imparting awareness was as follows. The NGO staff provided information on relevant schemes and programmes in weekly/ monthly meetings of SHGs or special training programmes conducted for this purpose. The schemes on which information provided included DWCRA, schemes by SC/ST Corporation, housing, sanitary facilities, loans for undertaking income generating activities, welfare schemes and loans for agricultural development. In general, most of the sample members were aware of IRDP programmes relating to basic amenities, and minimum needs such as old age pension. Of those members who came to know about these programmes, a majority could access the resources. The performance in terms of productive utilisation was even better. However, variations among the NGOs could be observed in terms of level of awareness, and proportion of members obtaining resources. An attempt to relate this information with NGO statements on need for interface, strategies adopted and problems faced did not provide meaningful pattern. To some extent, this could be explained in terms of comparative strength of NGOs. For instance, one of the NGOs placed considerable emphasis on mobilising DWCRA assistance to SHGs promoted as it was felt that the DWCRA grants would strengthen the ability of SHGs to meet the credit needs of members. Hence, levels of awareness and proportion of members obtaining the resources were high in the case of this NGO. But, the same was not true in the case of another, which placed even more emphasis on mobilisation of DWCRA grants.

In contrast, the proportion of members successfully utilising the resources provided by the government did not vary significantly across the NGO project areas. This suggests that once the SHG members obtained resources, they properly utilised the resources and retained the assets acquired with the help of these resources. Most of the members reported an increase in employment and income.

To a question whether members of SHG faced problems in approaching the government officials and in accessing the resources, it was learnt that only a small proportion of the members actually visited the government offices and met the concerned officials on their own due to the following. First, the government offices were distantly located, and hence, opportunity costs in terms of wage income forgone had come in the way of continuous follow-up to the offices. Second, the male members of their households often were not supportive of their visits to government offices. Third, the complicated procedures and indifferent attitude of the officials were cited as important problems by a few of the sample members. Fourth, a significant proportion of members stated that there was enormous delay between application and sanction, and sanction and disbursal. This was mainly due to lack of follow-up compounded by the problems of distant location and unsympathetic attitude of the male household members.

Interestingly, a large proportion of the sample members visited the government offices, but rarely interacted with government officials because of the following. First, the NGO itself mobilised the resources based on its reputation in the local area, and groundwork (in terms of dialogue meetings inviting the concerned officials to the project area, etc.) before mobilising the resources. Second, the NGO staff prepared the applications, submitted the same in the relevant office, followed up with concerned officials and obtained resources for the target group. Hence, sample members noted that there was no need to meet the concerned officials except when the assistance was actually provided to them.

The pattern on whether or not members visited the government offices could be related to the type of interface practised by NGOs. A few of the NGOs mobilised the resources on their own, and hence, did not make any significant efforts to involve the people in the interface process. This was done because the government departments themselves invited four of the NGOs to participate in the implementation of programmes such as sanitation, DWCRA and Income Generation programmes. The second group of the NGOs played a dominant role in the interface process as compared to the people, either because of survival concerns or pressures from the donor. The staff in these NGOs played a major role in the interface process to achieve targets set either by the NGO or donor. Three NGOs belonged to this category. The third type of NGOs made efforts to build the institutional capacity of the members, who were in the forefront as far as the interface process was concerned. Two NGOs belonged to this category. First category of NGOs is characterised by co-option, the second by collaboration and third by critical collaboration. Reorganisation of primary data (Tables 1.4 and 1.5) along these three categories provides meaningful patterns.

Table 1.4 provides information on levels of awareness, access and utilisation of government programmes among target group members by type of NGOs. An important finding has been that the level of awareness was in general high among target group members from the project areas of NGOs pursuing critical collaboration. These NGOs made dissemination of information as an important component of their programmes. Information was provided to the target group members in SHG meetings and special training programmes. On the other hand, the level of awareness among the target group members from the project areas of NGOs pursuing collaboration or characterised by co-option was less. Imparting awareness on the programmes was given less emphasis as the individual NGOs obtained government resources on their own strength or their own persuasion. Another important feature was that some of the members obtained information on these programmes through different channels such as local decentralised government or from the government directly.

There are also differences in so far as accessing the resources by the type of NGOs. In general, a larger proportion of target group members from the project areas of NGOs pursuing critical collaboration accessed resources as compared to the other two types. However, the difference is not significant, and in the case of a few programmes, a larger proportion of target group members from the NGOs characterised by co-option accessed the resources. But this

Table 1.4 : Levels of awareness, access and utilisation of the government programmes by the type of NGOs

Particulars	*NGOs characterised by*											
	Co-option			*Collaboration*			*Critical collaboration*			*All NGOs*		
	Aw	*Obtn*	*Utln*	*Aw*	*Obtn*	*Utln*	*Aw*	*Obtn*	*Utln*	*Aw*	*Obtn*	*Utln*
DWCRA	25.00	89.47	88.24	23.33	92.86	76.92	35.00	85.71	100.00	26.70	89.36	88.10
SC/ST Corporation Scheme	15.79	66.67	62.50	15.00	77.78	85.71	50.00	100.00	100.00	23.30	85.37	88.57
Land site for housing	25.00	52.63	20.00	30.00	55.56	100.00	65.00	69.23	77.78	35.80	60.32	68.42
Sanitary facilities, drinking water, PMRY, JRY	32.89	100.00	84.00	51.67	38.71	83.33	67.50	59.26	93.75	47.16	63.86	86.79
Loans to support rural artisans (TRYSEM, IRDP)	57.89	31.82	71.43	65.00	48.72	57.89	55.00	81.82	88.89	59.66	48.57	72.55
Schemes relating to OAP, education, hostel, electricity, family planning, widower pension, etc.	61.84	36.17	76.47	25.00	46.67	100.00	37.50	93.33	71.43	43.75	49.35	78.95
Loans to agriculture (tank desiltation, livestock, etc.)	31.58	75.00	83.33	45.00	92.59	72.00	57.50	47.83	100.00	42.05	72.97	81.48

Note : Aw : % of members aware of the programmes
Obtn : % of members obtaining the programmes
Utln : % of members productively utilising the programmes.

was mostly because the NGO was in the forefront in mobilising these resources from the government. When it came to productive utilisation of resources, the performance of the target group members from the project areas of NGOs pursuing critical collaboration was far better. This was because these NGOs gave utmost importance to build the capacity of members in productive utilisation of government resources as this would have a bearing on sustainable interface.

One of the NGOs prepared the target group in terms of providing training on business development. When the government sanctioned a scheme relating to individual sanitary facilities, the implementation was done through beneficiary committees, which ensured quality and cost-effectiveness.

Thus, although all types of NGOs succeeded in having interface between the target groups and government departments, the quality varied. The role of people was much less in the case of first two types of NGOs as compared to the third type. This would have an impact on the sustainability of the interface process.

Table 1.5 provides more conclusive evidence on the type of interface. More than two-thirds of members from the project areas of NGOs characterised by co-option stated that they depended on NGOs to obtain resources from the government. About one-fifth of members stated that they were independent in approaching the government officials and access the resources. The situation is significantly better in the case of NGOs pursuing collaboration.

Table 1.5 : Dependence (%) of target group on NGOs in approaching the government officials and accessing the resources

Particulars	*NGOs characterised by*			
	Co-option	*Collabo-ration*	*Critical collaboration*	*All NGOs*
Dependence on NGOs	64.47	43.33	17.50	46.60
Independent in approaching	21.05	38.33	62.50	36.40
Independent in the long run	10.53	18.00	20.00	15.30
Did not meet officials	3.95	0.00	0.00	1.70
Total	100	100	100	100
Actual	76	60	40	176

About 38 per cent stated that they became independent while less than one-fifth stated they were likely to become independent in the long run. In contrast, nearly two-thirds of target group members from the project areas of NGOs pursuing critical collaboration stated that they were independent. This was because the role of the people in establishing and sustaining the interface by undertaking the following activities had been stressed from the beginning in these programmes. Information on programmes was provided. Efforts to improve their capacity to approach the officials were made. The NGO staff was told to play a facilitative rather than a dominant role under which their own involvement gradually declined. Formats to monitor the process of interface were developed. These were reviewed in monthly meetings. Once the target group members obtained the resources, their utilisation and repayment of loans, if any, were monitored along with the leaders of SHGs. Because of this intensive process, the quality of interface process was different and potential to become sustainable.

CONCLUSIONS

The chapter sought to analyse the type of interface between the government, NGOs and people. The main conclusion is that of the nine NGOs, four are characterised by co-option, three by collaboration and two by critical collaboration. Thus, the dominant form of interface is either co-option or collaboration.

The NGOs characterised by co-option or collaboration chose their respective paths due to the pressure of donors or compulsions created out of an increase in the size of NGOs in terms of number of villages, groups and target group members. With uncertain donor environment, they were compelled to access the resources for their own survival or for the target group. When NGOs do not have autonomy in terms of funding or development vision, the co-option or collaboration seems to be the most likely outcome.

This type of interface has implications on people-centred development and sustainability. It appears that people's participation in true sense is not needed in collaboration or co-option. This has implications on the dependence of the target group on NGOs for establishing linkages with the government departments. If the NGOs become contractors or middle agencies between the government and people, there would always be questions on their accountability and the very purpose of this type of development.

Only two NGOs seem to be pursuing critical collaboration largely because of support that they received from donors in terms of vision development and continued funding support. Critical collaboration wherein the people gradually take control of the interface process is needed, but this has implications in terms of costs and benefits, and raises the questions such as 'who has to meet these costs' and 'for how long'.

Finally, if the government and donor agencies, consciously or unconsciously, push NGOs to follow the path of co-option or simple collaboration, the questions 'whether this is needed or not' and 'why efforts to change the attitude of development bureaucracy are not made instead of concentrating on NGO mediated interface' arise.

NOTES

1. These were formed by the educated, middle and lower middle class youth who were dissatisfied with the government programmes which widened the gap between the rich and the poor. These people were unhappy with the Left parties, which failed to consider the problems of the poorest (Fernandes 1985). Influenced by the Western Marxist thought, SAGs criticised that the government neither had the capacity nor the political will to improve the living standards of the poor.
2. However, many officials and members of NGOs were not enthusiastic about politicians setting up NGOs using their earlier connections (Sen 1999).
3. Launched by several developmental NGOs, CBOs, activists and intellectuals, the movement was mainly concerned with environment degradation and rehabilitation of people displaced by the Narmada project.
4. These were FCRA, Financial Act of 1983, banning foreign funding for NGOS involved in empowerment activities, removal of tax exemptions from all income generating activities of NGOs, etc. (Fernandes 1985; Jain 1986; Kothari 1986).
5. The term was coined by Wolch (1990) while analysing the state-non profit sector relations in the US and UK. A shadow state refers to a parastatal apparatus consisting of voluntary organisations charged with the responsibility of providing services, which, otherwise, would have been provided by the state.
6. These obtain project/programmes from government or donors either by competitive tendering or through sub-contracting on a non-competitive basis (Robinson 1997). These are non-profit organisations that provide service to the aid donors and governments for implementing development

programmes, and are often driven by market factors rather than the values and motives that are generally associated with the NGOs.

7. Federation of Voluntary Organisations for Rural Development in Karnataka (FEVORD-K) and VANI are examples of NGO networks.
8. The study of PRADAN (1996) states that many NGOs have used demonstration to influence the government officials.
9. This strategy has also been used elsewhere (Sethna and Shah 1993).

REFERENCES

Association for Voluntary Agencies for Rural Development (AVARD) (1992). *Government — NGO Interface in India's Development.* A Country Paper. Manila: *Asian NGO Coalition for Agrarian Sector and Rural Development.*

Bhat, K.V. and S. Satish (1993). NGO Links with the Karnataka State Watershed Development Cell: MYRADA and the PIDOW Project. In John Farrington *et al* (eds.), *Non-Governmental Organisation and the State in Asia: Rethinking Roles in Sustainable Agricultural Development.* London and New York: Routledge.

Chandhoke, N. and A. Ghosh (eds.) (1995). *Grass Roots Movements and Social Change. Delhi:* University of Delhi Press.

Chowdhary, Paul D. (1987). Critical Appraisal of Voluntary Effort in Social Welfare and Development since Independence. *The Indian Journal of Public Administration,* 33 (3): 492 - 500.

Edwards, Michael and David Hulme (eds.) (1995). *Non-Governmental Organisation—Performance and Accountability: Beyond the Magic Bullet.* London: Earthscan.

Fernandes, W. (1985). Introduction: Social Activities and the Search for Alternatives. In W. Fernandes (ed.), *Social Activities and People's Movement.* New Delhi: Indian Social Institute.

Jain, L.C. (1986). Debates in the Voluntary Sector: Some Reflections. *Social Action,* 36 (4): 404-16.

Korten, D.C. (1987). Third Generation NGO Strategies: A Key to People Centered Development. *World Development,* 15 (7-12) (Special Issue): 145-59.

Korten, D.C. (1990). *Getting to the Twenty-First Century: Voluntary Action and the Global Agenda.* West Hartford, CT: Kumarian Press.

Kothari, Rajni (1986). NGOs, the State and World Capitalism. *Economic and Political Weekly,* XXI (50): 2177-82.

Kudva, Neema (1996). *Uneasy Partnerships? Government-NGO Relations in India.* Department of City and Regional Planning, University of California at Berkeley. Mimeo.

Maheshwari, S. (1987). Voluntary Action in Rural Development in India. *The Indian Journal of Public Administration,* 33 (3): 559-68.

Mayoux, Linda and S. Johnson (1997). *Micro-finance and Women's Empowerment: Strategies for Increasing Impact.* A Report of the Workshop held during January 13-15, 1997, Addis Ababa, Ethiopia. London: Action Aid.

Murthy, R.K. and Nitya Rao (1997). *Indian NGOs, Poverty Alleviation and their Capacity Enhancement in the 1990s: An Institutional and Social Relations Perspective.* New Delhi: FES.

PRADAN (1996). *Towards a Relationship of Significance: Interim Report on the Study of Relationships between Government and NGOs in Rajasthan.* New Delhi: Professional Assistance for Development Action.

Rajasekhar, D. and Lini R. Nair (1995). Networks among NGDOs in Karnataka. In D. Rajasekhar *et al.* (eds.), *People Centered Rural Development: NGDOs and Decentralised Government.* Bangalore: ISEC, CDR, NOVIB and BCO.

Rajasekhar, D. and Narasimha Reddy (1997). *Local Development Programmes and NGOs: A Guide on Local and State Government Programmes for Fieldworkers.* Bangalore: BCO and NOVIB.

Ramachandran, Vimal A. (1995). Equality among Unequal Parties: Relationship between NGOs and Government. *The Administrator,* XL: 119-28.

Reddy, N.L. Narasimha and D. Rajasekhar (1996). *Development Programmes and NGOs: A Guide on Central Government Programmes for NGOs in India.* Bangalore: BCO and NOVIB.

Robinson, M. (1997). Privatising the Voluntary Sector: NGOs as Public Service Contractors. In D. Hulme and M. Edwards (eds.), *NGOs, State and Donors: Too Close for Comfort.* New York: St. Martin's Press, Inc.

Sen, Siddhartha (1999). Some Aspects of State NGO Relationships in India in the Post-Independence Era. *Development and Change,* 30 (2): 327-55.

Sethna, A. and Anil Shah (1993). The Agha Khan Rural Support Project (AKRSP): Influencing Waste Land Development Policy. In John Farrington *et al.* (eds.), *Non-Governmental Organisation and the State in Asia: Rethinking Roles in Sustainable Agricultural Development.* London and New York: Routledge.

Tandon, Rajesh and David Brown (1990). *The Evolution of the Development Sector in India: An Overview Report.* New Delhi: Society for Participatory Research in Asia. Mimeo.

Unia, P. (1991). Social Action Group Strategies in the Indian Sub-Continent. *Development in Practice,* 1 (2): 84-96

Webster, Neil (1995). A Conceptual Approach to NGDOs and Panchayat Raj in Rural Development. In D. Rajasekhar *et al.* (eds.), *People Centered Rural Development: NGDOs and Decentralised Government.* Bangalore: ISEC, CDR, NOVIB and BCO.

Wolch, J.R. (1990). *The Shadow State: Government and the Voluntary Sector in Transition.* New York: The Foundation Centre.

2

Institutional Framework for Poverty Alleviation in Krishna and Nalgonda Districts of Andhra Pradesh

PATRICK KRAUSE

INTRODUCTION

Improving the living conditions of the poorest sections of society cannot be done in an isolated and *ad hoc* manner. The multifaceted nature of poverty requires any development practitioner to approach the issue in a holistic way integrating different activities as well as different actors. Understanding the specific institutional framework for poverty alleviation in a given sectoral or geographical area has to be the starting point for any activity towards sustainable poverty alleviation.

This chapter concentrates on the institutional framework for poverty alleviation as a major component of the specific environment in two districts of Andhra Pradesh, namely, Nalgonda and Krishna. In each of the districts, a variety of actors are involved in poverty alleviation. Getting a grasp of the diverse and complementary strengths and limitations of the different actors in their quest to improve the living conditions of the poor as well as of the linkages and relations between each other is the main aim of the this chapter.

There are three main actors involved in establishing institutional framework for poverty alleviation: (1) government organisations; (2) institutional credit agencies (Co-operative Credit Societies,

Commercial Banks and Regional Rural Banks); and (3) NGOs. Among them the government is perceived as the most dominant player in initiating the development process. Most of the development programmes are designed at the national/state level and passed on to a district for implementation. In terms of financial resources as well as personnel and political power, government organisations take a lead in the development process of the country.

Institutional credit agencies are also important partners in the development process as they co-finance most of the existing government programmes and also have been directly lending to the poor in recent years through the linkage programme of NABARD. Lastly, NGOs have been recognised by some development practitioners and academicians as particularly successful in reaching the poor. Yet most of the Indian NGOs have very limited scope and have failed to establish systematic linkages between their work at the grass roots level and the broader framework that shapes their activities.

Based on these general assumptions, the central questions behind the analysis are :

- What are the specific strengths and limitations of the different actors?
- How can one utilise the specific strengths of different actors to improve the living conditions of the poor?
- What are the opportunities to improve and strengthen the relations between different actors in order to improve the quality and effectiveness of the services to the poor?
- How can the strategic linkages between different actors be built up?
- How can a critical and constructive dialogue between different actors be established?
- How can this process be initiated and institutionalised?

In order to answer these questions, semi-structured interviews were conducted with district government officials, bankers and NGOs: A conscious effort was made to include the key actors[1] at the district level. Interviews were also held with some branch officers of commercial banks about their experience in poverty alleviation activities and a variety of NGOs.

The questionnaire, which was framed depending on the experiences and responsibilities of key actors, focused on: concepts of poverty and self-help; interventions and strategies; and cooperation between the actors to obtain the conceptual clarity of different actors. In this context, answers were also sought on the following questions: how do they perceive poverty and what self-help means to them; can and do the actors shape the implementation of their activities? How do different actors co-operate and relate to each other and whether there is any scope to institutionalise the co-operation between different actors?[2]

Concepts of poverty and self-help

The definition of poverty is not only an academic exercise, but also, more importantly, it reveals the perception of an individual or institution of poverty and the approach to alleviate it. Among government officials there was great variation in the answers to this question. Some had a very sound understanding of poverty and included issues such as basic needs, powerlessness, dignity and equity in their definition. In one case, Robert Chambers was quoted as the starting point for the definition of poverty. One official referred to the gender dimensions of poverty, i.e., dependency and lack of opportunities and rights. In most cases, poverty was understood as insufficient basic needs including lack of food, shelter, health and education. Lack of education was frequently emphasised as a major problem.

One influential official did not see much of an issue here, as "we don't have any problem of getting the minimum food. We do not have any famines". The same official stated in a foreword to a major planning document for the district that a "majority of its (the districts) population lives below the poverty line. Under such circumstances, it should be the endeavour of both the bankers and development agencies to strive hard to implement the anti-poverty and self-employment schemes of the government to ameliorate the economic conditions of the poor and needy". This is an example of a flagrant discrepancy between the written and the spoken word of officials. Another official defined poverty as "due to irregular seasonal conditions".

The perception of poverty among the government officials differs extremely and depends on individual involvement or commitment. There is no clear pattern to it, i.e., it cannot be argued that higher ranking district officials have a better understanding of the concept than others.

There was a difference in understanding the concept of poverty between the district level representatives and the branch managers. The former defined poverty as lack of food, shelter and low annual income. In one case, a manager stated that "poverty needs to be experienced". He also added lack of political awareness as an important point concentrated on lack of physical assets. Overall, however, the definitions concentrated on lack of physical assets.

The branch managers again can be divided into managers of Regional Rural Banks (RRBs) and commercial banks. The rural bank branch managers seemed highly committed to the poverty alleviation goal. Poverty was defined in almost emotional terms such as 'a skeleton working'. In the commercial banks, on the contrary, poverty was perceived as caused by laziness: "when I go to the villages I see all these men hanging around doing nothing all day". NGOs emphasise the social dimensions of poverty more than the other actors. They not only include lack of basic needs but also stress the point that poor are socially excluded from the development process and powerless in their ways to overcome their miserable position. This can only be achieved by a certain degree of capacity building through external support.

Concepts of self-help and self-help promotion are widely used by the Indian government institutions, banks and NGOs alike. Across the government as well as the banking institutions, it can be found that the concept of self-help is quite strongly linked to SHGs and their performance. In general, self-help seems to have a firm collective connotation. A government official, for instance, defined it as 'thinking together'.

Many government officials complain about the expectations of the people. In this respect, self-help means the opposite of waiting for the government to deliver services. Only recently there have been some efforts from the government to define self-help as the basis for the formation of the Development of Women and Children in Rural Areas (DWCRA) groups or *SAMABHAVANA* groups, as they are called in Nalgonda District. In Nalgonda District, it was stated that the DWCRA scheme was not very successful until 1995, precisely because of lack of definition of self-help. It is only for the last year or two that a sound self-help strategy is being followed.

The most refined definition of self-help was given by one district official in Nalgonda. To him, self-help meant, "that people should stand on their own feet and generate their own resources. Initially, some government support might be needed for that, but after some time the government should withdraw". This, however, was the only example where self-help was detached from a group concept and a long-term vision was given.

Bankers, on the other hand, tie their concept of self-help exclusively to the SHGs and their performance in savings and credit activities. Bank managers, at least, at the district level have recognised the potential in Banking with the poor and they are very much interested in the expansion of the linkage programme in both the districts. Bank officials seem to have a clear-cut agenda when it comes to self-help and its promotion. Recovering loans, meeting targets and making profits are the key notions in their programme. These goals can only be achieved if people come together regularly to solve their own problems in sustainable manner. In both the districts, the institutional credit agencies make a conscious effort to teach their branch officers about the self-help concept. They take up exposure programmes and organise workshops. The Indian Bank in Krishna, for example, made it compulsory for all the branch managers to visit at least one SHG during their training.

While one can notice a uniform understanding of self-help, i.e., SHGs, and lending to the poor at the district level, the perceptions of the branch managers at the lower levels are very much divided. Branch managers had no experience with group lending and were also lacking an understanding of the basic group concept: "if one person cannot repay, how can a group? Fifteen people taken together are 15 times worse". In another case, the branch manager had bad experience with group lending even though he had never practised it before nor had he been exposed to any group lending activities (the groups will start fighting). Interestingly, this was a branch of Canara Bank, which is the most successful commercial bank in linking SHGs in Andhra Pradesh, supporting 456 SHGs with a loan volume of more than Rs.1 crore (see, NABARD 1998e).

The RRB officers, on the contrary, have been found to have a better understanding of the SHGs. They have grasped the group concept and they have also understood that lending to SHGs can improve the recovery rate and thus, can be good business also. In this context, one needs to investigate further how the obvious difference between RRBs and commercial banks comes about.

Many NGOs have a very strong self-help concept. Self-help promotion often is a major component of their everyday work. According to the NGOs, helping people to help themselves requires proper response to local needs and initiatives and also facilitate the process to overcome poverty. This leads to a broader definition of self-help and self-help promotion than any of the other actor has put forward.

Interventions and strategies

When it came to the main problems within the district, most of the officials in Krishna District gave a controversial picture of the prosperous and well-irrigated eastern part and a backward, underdeveloped poorly irrigated upland area. In Nalgonda, no such clear divide exists and accordingly, the answers varied greatly.

In both the districts, it was difficult to get a quick and comprehensible overview by the government officers of the main activities in their own departments. Some of the officers gave a brief description of their operations. It was, however, incredibly hard to get basic written information in any of the offices. Even though the officials mentioned studies, action plans and other papers they had prepared for the department, none of the material was readily available.

The information that was accessible was mostly on financial targets and whether they had been met or not. There were no summary reports on the various government schemes in the district, the ways they linked up with, supplemented and complemented each other, the status of the schemes, the resources spent, the mechanisms of allocation of these resources, the impact, etc. As far as the allocation of resources was concerned, there were different mechanisms in place. The resources for infrastructure, for instance, were given to the blocks on an equal footing by the Government of India (GOI). This created difficulties, as some areas need infrastructure more than others did. The resources could not be used according to the needs without violating the regulations, as one official stated. For the Watershed Programme, the Central Government allocated the resources according to the needs *via* the Remote Sensing Agency at

Hyderabad. Direct poverty alleviation programmes, such as IRDP, were supposed to be entirely under the control of the district administration.

Some of the government officials saw scope for strategising the schemes for development. In one case, emphasis was laid on the more promising schemes. Most officials referred to a targetting mechanism, which was, however, somewhat confusing and lacked transparency. Furthermore, the available documents only gave financial targets and achievements.

A few government officials quite clearly expressed that there was no room for manoeuvre. They saw themselves as employees of the government, appointed to implement the existing programmes. "I am only the custodian of the money", as one official put it.

The monitoring and evaluation mechanisms of development programmes were not developed. According to the officials, these mechanisms varied from evaluations by external agencies to regular seminars and workshops, keeping a close contact with the villagers, to touring the district and conducting grievance days to get acquainted with the views of the people. One official stated that the resources were not available for a meaningful monitoring and evaluation of a scheme.

In general, the officials were remarkably uncritical about the performance of the direct poverty alleviation programmes considering the obvious and widely recognised weaknesses of the schemes[3]. Only on very rare occasions did government officials doubt the efficacy of the direct poverty alleviation programmes (Box 2.1).

Box 2.1 : The performance of government programmes as stated by the officials
• Generally misplaced services • Failing to reach the poorest of the poor • Ignoring the immediate consumption needs of the poorest • High transaction costs for the poorest • Political interference • Lack of service motives in government officials • Corruption

In the offices of the bankers, information and materials were readily available. The Potential Linked Credit Plan (PLCP), the Annual Credit Plan or the Service Area Credit Plan were first made available in the district bank offices. From these plan documents one could get an idea of the focal areas of the bank activities and the major strategies adopted within a given period. Furthermore, evaluation reports, strategy papers and even some DRDA materials were obtainable here.

In general, the banks were not very satisfied with co-financing government programmes as the recovery rate was extremely bad in Nalagonda district. Their major future thrust in the area of poverty alleviation was clearly on the linkage programme. For this, they set clear targets, and concrete steps were taken to achieve these targets also. Banks were assessing SHGs, organising exposure and training programmes and workshops and they started identifying credible NGOs who could be employed for the linkage programme. Furthermore, in rhetoric as well as on paper, banks showed keen interest in reaching the poorest. "In one-third of the district, poverty is still prevailing, we need to target our interventions", a banker in Krishna stated.

Despite the efforts, the idea of linking SHGs to the banks seems to be still quite fresh to the bank managers. In Nalgonda, no direct lending to SHGs has taken place so far. In Krishna District, the first direct loan to a SHG has only been released after a long struggle between NGOs and the banks a few months ago. The ideas have also not trickled down to the branch managers yet.

Most of the NGOs were very clear about their objectives and about the strategy employed to achieve them. As they were limited in size and scope, it was an easy task for them to present their activities in a nutshell. Also, the objectives and strategies of a NGO were usually worked out by the NGO itself. The directors, secretaries, the staff themselves developed the ideas and, thus, identified with it.

Cooperation between different actors

Within the district there are a variety of departments, which share the responsibility for poverty alleviation. Out of them, the DRDA takes a key position with the largest poverty alleviation schemes by coordinating or organising the various development activities and poverty alleviation programmes within the district. For those officials who are, in general, very uncritical of their own performance, this coordination process works smoothly. For others, it depends on individuals and most importantly, on the collector as he or she is the pivotal of the district. All the strings are pulled together in the person of the collector. But also, the attitude of other district officials can hinder or foster the coordination process. Some influential officials complained about employees who were comfortable with their position and salary, lacking service motive.

In various cases, considerable gaps in the coordination process were identified. The DRDA, for example, "has no authority over related departments". Moreover, the mandal level officials, through whom a major part of the DRDA work is executed and on whom the success of the implementation depends, are not answerable to the Project Director. One person mentioned lack of efficiency in the cooperation between different government departments and avoidable overlaps. In one case, the same training was provided to the same group by two different departments in consecutive years.

In both the districts, there are a variety of linkages between NGOs and the administration through government programmes and personal contacts. In Nalgonda, NGOs are involved in the Pulse Polio Campaign and Family Planning programme. Two NGOs are employed as project implementing agencies for the Watersheds. Three NGOs are involved in the Joint Forest Management (JFM) programme. In Krishna District, the involvement of NGOs goes a step further. Recently, the District Collector invited some NGOs to take on the implementation of a Water and Sanitation Awareness Campaign (WASAN) with a self-help promotion perspective. In addition to this, the NGOs are conducting a training programme for cluster volunteers on self-help promotion for the whole district. A similar programme for officers of different government departments has been planned. Another idea that has come up is to start a newsletter on government-NGO cooperation.

In the programmes, NGOs are usually not involved in the design and planning of the activities. Only after the framework of the scheme is finalised that the NGOs are called upon for the implementation of the scheme. In Nalgonda, some NGOs came into being only after the Watershed Programme was started. This meant that they did not even have an agenda of their own but functioned merely as implementing agency. The cooperation between the two players is quite often based on project guidelines. NGOs then "should follow the guidelines" as one official put it.

Apart from the Watershed programme, where NGOs have to be involved, the exchange between government departments and NGOs works mostly at the individual level. In both the districts, NGOs do occasionally build up good contacts with open and committed government officials. The contacts are highly personalised in nature, though. As soon as the committed government officials are transferred to another post, as it happens very frequently, the rapport building process has to start afresh.

Government officials see the strengths of NGOs in their commitment, good rapport with the people and their success in training and guidance. These are the criteria they would employ for assessing NGOs. Box 2.2 presents a summary of the expectations that the government officials have.

There is still an atmosphere of mutual distrust between NGOs and the government departments. Government officials are seen as corrupt, adhering to inflexible, bureaucratic structures. The system, in general, is "failing to serve the poor and needy". NGOs, on the other hand, lack accountability and often integrity. Their activities fall short of showing any impact. According to one official: "we have formed 7,000 groups, NGOs have done 20, may be 30....the impact doesn't show at the district level. If those groups (the NGO-groups) can be said to be the best or if they have saved a lot of money or been successful in taking up economic activities, I would say they have made an impact". This statement indicates that NGO activities do not have much impact at the district level. One official clearly stated that he would prefer to work with the people directly. "Our entire programme is driven by motivators who are local persons, the local youths or women......A local youth from the village is more useful to me than the NGO". This ensures that the services reach the poor and have a larger impact as committed individuals at the local level are always available.

Box 2.2: What do government officials expect from NGOs?
• NGOs should follow the guidelines, whatever the objective of the programme is. • Monitoring, guidance and training. • Development of good rapport with the people. • Empowerment of the village community. • Motivating the people. • NGOs should be non-biased and non-political. • NGOs should be a 'helping-hand'. • NGOs should have better contacts with the grass roots. • NGOs should have strong grass roots-orientation and integrity. • NGOs should be self-sustained, active in social mobilisation and have a strong commitment. • NGOs should have community organisation, capacity for empowerment and skill improvement. • Monitoring and evaluation should always be done by the NGOs.

The exchange between governments and NGOs appears to be based on a donor-recipient relationship rather than realising each other's potential. On one occasion, a government official asked why an NGO needed to co-operate with the administration when they got their funding from a donor agency. So far, there is no systematic exchange between the two actors. There are no regular meetings or a platform for dialogue. The government has neither a list of NGOs nor track records of their activities.

Both NGOs and government officials have not taken any active step to foster an institutionalised relationship and opinions are divided over this issue. One official argued that he would not like to see the relationship institutionalised as this would open the doors to all kinds of NGOs regardless of their credibility. He preferred the existing situation to continue. Whenever he needed NGOs, he could call upon some dedicated organisations that he had built good rapport with. Other officials stated that they would encourage a process of institutionalisation and invite NGOs to think about it. One official suggested to clearly demarcate the areas or sectors of cooperation to avoid unhealthy competition and confusion. One NGO in Nalgonda made an effort to keep government officials informed about its activities by way of submitting monthly progress reports on SHGs to the DRDA. But, this is not a widespread phenomenon.

Even when there are government officials who are interested in stronger cooperation, there is a visible gap between them and the NGOs. "We need the involvement of NGOs. Mostly we approach them, but they rarely come to us". Another official would welcome to have a list of credible NGOs for involving them in development activities. Many NGOs seem to be doubtful about linkages with the government. They need government funding and take up government schemes but want to work independently. Some NGOs see their role *vis-a-vis* the government as advocates in favour of the downtrodden. Government schemes often fail to serve their objectives and the NGOs should give the right inputs to make the delivery services work more efficiently. They have to be careful not to be abused for implementation purposes. One NGO visualised the relationship as organised meetings in which they could concentrate on strategic inputs.

There is a long distance from sporadic exchange to a critical and constructive dialogue. "As long as they (NGOs) talk sense they will be taken seriously". This, however, can only "happen after some time. Now we are in a transition period". A critical collaboration between the two actors is only possible if NGOs are independent. 'As long as they rely on funds from the government they cannot have a voice', as one official framed it.

Bank managers at the district level are, in general, very open for co-operation with the NGOs and they see a clear role for them also. "We want the cooperation with NGOs to a maximum extent ... To stabilise the system we need the co-operation of the NGOs. There is no second opinion about it". The banks themselves have no sufficient time and resources to form the groups and guide them properly. This is the main area where they like to see more NGO involvement (see Box 2.3). The banks have come to realise that SHGs formed by NGOs function better than groups formed by the government agencies. A major aim of the linkage programme is to combine "the flexibility, sensitivity and responsiveness of the informal credit system with the strength of technical and administrative capabilities and financial resources of the formal financial institutions" (NABARD 1998d).

Again NGOs are mere silent partners in that relationship. Banks have taken steps from their side to collect information on NGOs. While a study of SHGs in Nalgonda District conducted in April

1998 reveals that "it is gathered that one or two NGOs functioning in the district are helping with the formation of SHGs and their perpetuation ..." (NABARD 1998c), and the PLCP finalised only a few months later lists six NGOs with altogether 409 SHGs (NABARD 1998a).

Box 2.3 : What do banks expect from NGOs?

- Credibility.
- Should be "long-term players".
- Should be dedicated to the upliftment of the poor.
- NGOs are wanted on the training programme for bankers.
- Form well-functioning groups.
- Provide training to the groups.
- Act as facilitators and monitors.
- NGOs should withdraw their activities at some point and move to another area where poverty still persists (withdrawal strategy).

Bankers see the identification of credible NGOs as their problem in the process. To tackle this issue, NABARD has developed an assessment format to collect information on suitable NGOs to work with. In both districts, the managers had prepared lists of NGOs, which were the starting point for this endeavour—53 NGOs in Krishna and 72 NGOs in Nalgonda. District representatives encouraged their branch managers to approach the NGOs in their area of operation, attend meetings of SHGs and personally analysed how the groups were functioning to make up their mind.

Some NGOs are, according to the district managers, not interested in linking up with the bank. Either they are scared that involving banks may spoil the people or they have their own institutional interests. Quite a few NGOs have their own revolving funds or they are involved in the Rashtriya Mahila Kosh (RMK), functioning as financial intermediaries. The bank managers are mostly interested in NGOs as facilitators. They do not want to lend to NGOs but rather release the loans directly to the target groups. In one case, misuse of funds was reported.

Apart from this, banks have had good experience with NGOs. They mainly use NGOs for exposure purposes to make bankers aware of SHGs and their functioning. Compared to Nalgonda, the exchange between banks and NGOs progressed well in Krishna District. Here, some NGOs advised bankers on the curriculum for an SHG-training unit. In Krishna, the Assistant General Manager of NABARD has taken branch managers to groups of some NGOs to familiarise them. Presently, a training scheme for the branch officers in the district is being planned. In Nalgaonda, a workshop on SHG-bank linkages for bankers, field level functionaries and voluntary agencies has been conducted for the first time.

District level officials welcome the process of institutionalisation. They appear to have a keen interest in institutionalising the exchange with carefully chosen NGOs. For this, they want NGOs to come forward and get engaged. Those NGOs which are involved in enabling the target groups to get access to credit facilities are highly dependent on the branch officers at the lower levels. Quite often, these branch officers lack a basic understanding of the SHG-concept and are highly suspicious about lending to the poor. One officer even stated that NGOs were "clubs for enjoyment", that "make business". It is here that strategic linkages are most obviously missing.

As for the relations between banks and government institutions, one interesting aspect emerged in the interviews. The bankers operating in the district were opposed to subsidies linked programmes. For these programmes, the repayment rate is traditionally very low. Therefore, the bankers were highly sceptical about any government involvement in the linkage programme. 'Government groups are not up to the mark'. As soon as the government comes in, people start expecting services free of cost, they neglect the repayment of loans and the SHG-concept gets distorted. Nevertheless, they are obliged to co-operate with the government and the government is also the major promoter of SHGs in the districts. Thus, bankers would like to see the government only to form the groups. Subsequently, they would come in to provide the loans, getting directly involved with the SHGs. Here, a clear strategy is still lacking on how to provide training and monitoring for these groups.

Linkages (Table 2.1) among NGOs are rather scanty. Only in June 1998 that 68 NGOs in Krishna District came together to discuss their ideas on poverty, self-help and self-help promotion and decided to form a 4 member committee which was to prepare an approach paper on a possible cluster in the district. This was the first time that the NGOs met to tackle a common task. Besides, one NGO was working on an assessment of the NGOs in the district for which some criteria were developed.

In addition, linkages exist between NGOs and government officials in Krishna. The WASAN-programme as well as the training programme for the cluster volunteers held jointly with the DRDA are examples. While some NGOs saw a contradiction between taking up the programme and bringing forward the NGO cluster, the WASAN-programme was perceived as a departure point for further collaboration among NGOs.

In Nalgonda, no such linkages NGOs are visible so far. There is exchange between NGOs and the government on the Watershed Programme and also collaboration on certain issues, but there has been no attempt to focus to tackle shared difficulties. NGOs are still operating in isolation and maintaining their independence.

Table 2.1 : Identified linkages between NGOs and other actors

Actors	*Krishna*	*Nalgonda*
Government	• Pulse polio campaign • Watershed • JFM • WASAN-programme • Training programme for relevant officials in planning	• Pulse polio campaign • • JFM • Family planning
Banks	• Curriculum development for training on SHG • Exposure programmes • Common workshops	• Common workshops
NGOs	• Cluster in progress • Training programme for cluster volunteers • Training programme for relevant officials in planning • WASAN—programme	• Sporadic exchange around different issues

While cooperation between the government and NGOs depends on a few programmes and personal relations, bank managers are strategically working on a stronger interaction with the NGOs. They appear to have a vision for this process. NGOs, among themselves, are still reluctant to join forces and link up with the banks although there is need for such a step.

Differences between the two districts

Most of the findings are similar across the two districts. The only difference, which can be seen, results from the highly individualised perception of poverty and self-help among government officials as well as the equally individualised personal linkages between the administration and the NGOs. Depending on whether the key officials are open for cooperation with the NGOs, it will be more or less easy to build up a dialogue with the government but it depends on the expansion.

As for the relation between government and the NGOs one can discern a clear difference across the two districts. In Nalgonda, NGOs still operate in isolation, while steps were taken to join forces in Krishna District. Besides, the NGO links to the administration appear to be stronger in Krishna. Here, NGOs train DWCRA cluster volunteers and government employees on the concepts of self-help and self-help promotion. This is a major influence.

Apart form being dependent on individual ties, the difference is also likely to be connected to the varying patterns of evolution of the NGO movements in the two districts. In Krishna, many of the NGOs came into existence after the devastating cyclone in 1977. Initially, they were occupied with relief activities. Afterwards, they moved on to rehabilitation work and finally, got more involved in development activities. Thus, many of the NGOs in Krishna have more than 20 years experience and are today mainly working on development issues.

Nalgonda District is known for a strong Naxalite movement in the 60s and the 70s. In the 70s, CROSS (an NGO) started operating in Nalgonda, basing their activities on the *Sangha* concept, a village level union movement. After 1985, CROSS disintegrated into splinter groups and collapsed. It was only in the beginning of the 90s that a new generation of NGOs emerged, which were active on development issues. The Pulse Polio Campaign was the first step to the government administration to involve NGOs in their activities. Even though NGOs operated for a few decades in Nalgonda, the government officials repeatedly emphasised that they were not very experienced : "you must realise that the NGOs are very young. They have only been formed 3 years ago. They still have to be trained." The officials clearly regard only the new generation of NGOs which focus on development activities as organisations they consider worth co-operating with.

Thus, it can be argued that well-experienced service delivery organisation which are apolitical (this is also one of the expectations of the government officials which is listed in Box 2.2) have better opportunities when it comes to linkages with the government, whereas, in Krishna, NGOs have taken first step to build up horizontal linkages. Such attempts are missing in Nalgonda District.

Identified gaps

From the results presented so far some gaps (Table 2.2) emerge which have to be investigated further if services for the poor are to be improved. Firstly, there is an obvious lack of conceptual clarity about poverty and self-help promotion among some government officials and among bank officials at the town levels with the government administration, and it depends to a great degree on the individual commitment of the official. Bankers have a good understanding at the district level but it fails to trickle down to the branch officers.

The vision and strategy for development and poverty alleviation are rather vague among a good number of district government officials. With government activities for poverty alleviation one can easily get the impression that they consist of a huge accumulation of different schemes designed and planned at the macro-level by the state or central government institutions, which are merely handed down to the district level for implementation. How the different programmes link up with each other and what kind of philosophy stands behind them remains mysterious.

Table 2.2: Concepts and strategies of various players at different levels

Levels	*Government*	*Banks*	*NGOs*
Macro-Level (National/State)	National and state level concepts and strategies (i.e., 5 year plan)	NABARD prepares the guidelines for banking with the poor	
Macro-Level (District)	Lack of conceptual clarity and visible strategic approach	Conceptual clarity, clear targets and action plans	
Micro-Level (Mandal/Village)		Clear difference between RRBs and commercial Banks	Good concepts and strategies but limited in scope

Many government officials are very uncritical about the performance of various schemes even though it is widely known that it is fairly poor. This goes hand in hand with unspecific targetting, monitoring and evaluation methods. The departments mostly work with financial targets and achievements. Quality criteria are completely missing. There is a clear lack of transparency about the programmes, the availability and status of schemes and the way in which resources are being allocated and the poor are being targetted. In the government offices, reading material is hardly ever accessible. NGOs lack information material. Most of the programmes take the form of a delivery system. This feeds a culture of expectations among the target groups. They take whatever is available to them without being able to influence the design and planning of the programmes.

There is lack of continuity in the relations between government institutions and NGOs. The exchange is at present highly dependent on a few government programmes, for which NGO involvement, individual contacts and links are required. As officers are transferred frequently, and priorities are often reset, continuous relations between NGOs and the government become impossible.

In that environment the transaction costs for the exchange between NGO and government institutions as well as between the target group and government institutions become very high. A lot of time and money have to be spent in the interaction with each other especially for the people, when they 'run around government offices'. For NGOs and the community alike this means detraction from the actual task. NGOs appear to be very passive in the exchange process with administration and banks. The interested bankers and government officials have to approach the NGOs. This also leads to a situation in which the others define the terms of reference and NGOs join in only later. NGOs are sceptical about linking up with the government as they are concerned about their independence, yet they are dependent on government funds and cooperation in their activities.

In some cases where NGOs make an effort to build up linkages with other institutions, follow-up is missing which makes the interaction difficult.

Most NGOs face complications in their interactions with government institutions. They are aware of the shortcomings of government interventions. Besides, they realise that they are too weak to face the administration and that they have to improve their bargaining position to really make a change. Nevertheless, they fail to set up horizontal linkages.

Because of the lack of continuous interaction a vacuum between the different actors prevails, which is naturally filled with distrust. Only rarely do the actors make any effort to overcome this gap and build trust. Especially, NGOs and the government fail to understand that they can combine their individual strengths to improve the services to the poor. Rather than identifying complementary skills an atmosphere of competition is felt. In some cases, the different actors fall short of understanding the other's limitations. This raises wrong expectations.

Conclusions and recommendations

For NGOs, a fundamental ambiguity prevails. On the one hand, they have to lobby for the target groups at government offices to improve the services and make their voices heard. On the other hand, they are in desperate need for funding and in this way also dependent on government support. Without self-autonomy, however, critical collaboration can hardly be achieved. This obliges NGOs to give some attention to ways and methods to generate their own resources and establish certain degree of independence (Box 2.4).

"There is need for NGOs to come forward and prove themselves", as one official put it. If NGOs do not want to be co-opted as purely implementing agencies they have to start becoming active with regard to building up linkages. Instead of donors, banks and government institutions defining the relations and the terms of reference, NGOs should set their own standards. This can best be done together. Institutionalisation of linkages with the government and the banks has to start among NGOs themselves. Many NGOs have to struggle with the same difficulties in their day-to-day operations. Yet, they rarely get together and exchange on their commonly identified problems. NGOs preach the philosophy of organisation to their target groups because marginalised groups have to join forces to make their voices heard but they themselves remain in isolation, striving hard to maintain their individuality (Box 2.4).

NGOs should have some knowledge of other like-minded NGOs in the area. They should be chosen according to their own criteria (quality). Also they should compile a list of other NGOs in the area containing information on where they operate, what sectors and objectives they have and how they are going about in achieving the objectives. They also need to define their roles and strengths *vis-a-vis* other actors and define the ways in which they want to interact with each other and the outside world. A more intensive exchange between NGOs will also lead to a process of horizontal learning.

Box 2.4 : Strengths and weaknesses of different actors

Actors	*Strengths*	*Weaknesses*
Government	• Coverage. • Legitimacy. • Wide range of government schemes. • Some committed individuals, etc.	• Lack of conceptual clarity. • Unspecific vision and strategy. • Vague targetting, monitoring and evaluation. • Target chasing as strategy. • Lack of transparency, information flow and publicity systems. • High fluctuations among district officials. • Lack of knowledge about NGOs. • Poor synergies between different departments, etc.
Banks	• Clear concepts and cstrategies • Business motives. • Coverage • Actively looking for cooperation with NGOs etc.	• Ideas fail to trickle down to the branch managers. • Inability to provide linkages. • Poor synergies between banks and governments institutions. • Recovery rate as the major criterion, etc.
NGOs	• Conceptual clarity • Clear strategies • Commitment towards poverty alleviation. • Good rapport with the people etc.	• Lack of transparency. • Limited in scope. • Operating in isolation. • Passivity in cooperation with other actors. • Fail to market themselves etc.

A conscious effort or a strategy to build trust between the various actors is essential for any interaction. Here, a form of mutual understanding is essential, which is based on awareness about the other players' views and positions as well as strengths and limitations. For example, it makes no sense to speak to a banker about this social obligation or expect him to be an activist. Rather, the tactic should be to understand the system in which he is functioning and demonstrate to him that lending to SHGs can be good business. Similarly, governments cannot expect a single NGO to make a wide impact in the district. This requires that one should be able to take the other person's chair.

Governments often fall short of providing other players in the field with necessary space to act out their strengths. Not every individual and organisation on the stage is obliged to support the government administration in their duties. Rather other players might have crucial assets, which should be supported by the government to improve the situation of the target groups.

A further strategy for trust building is maintenance of a high degree of transparency. Governments could think of setting up publication office where any interested individual or organisation can obtain basic information material without battling with bureaucratic hurdles. NGOs could also keep government departments and banks informed of their activities, progress and constraints on a regular basis.

In general, NGOs are very weak in selling themselves. A marketing strategy is not only for business but also for some of the strengths which NGOs are known for and are not mentioned by the government officials. Furthermore, many NGOs have a good concept of self-help. Put together this can be a useful and valuable input for government officials as will as bankers. Like government institutions, none of the NGOs have any information material on their activities. Actively selling an organisation is a method of proving its credibility and also a way to build trust with clients, donors and other partners. Government as well as banks need to make greater efforts to employ quality criteria for the evaluation of their work. The impact of the DWCRA group can neither be measured by the number of groups formed nor by the number of groups active. Rather it should be assessed whether the group members are from the poor target groups and whether the DWCRA-grouping improves the living standards of the women.

In this respect more research on development interventions and their impact as well as on the obstacles to use the existing resources is needed. Here, linking up with research institutions, conducting more pragmatic and praxis-oriented research would go a long way and add to the credibility for an intervention.

Linkages between different actors mean, first and foremost, an improvement in the access to services for the target groups. People's needs are more important than any institution's opportunities. Therefore, one of the major aims should be to ensure that people's perspectives are integrated into the planning and design of schemes and activities of different institutions.

Andhra Pradesh is highly conducive to self-help promotion and people's participation. The state government has set clear targets in favour of participation and empowerment of the people. Most of the

NGOs have the same objectives in their work which make them a vital overlap between the two institutions. In this regard, the focus needs to be on scaling up of the poorest sections of society rather than the scaling up of NGOs.

NOTES

1. These were District Collector, Project Director, DRDA, Executive Director, SC/ST-Corporation, Chairman, Zilla Panchayat, Assistant General Manager, NABARD, and the Manager of the Lead Bank.
2. Despite discussions with all the key actors in the district administration, the results of this study should not be taken as representative. They provide only a cross-cutting picture of the institutional framework within the districts, the activities of and the relations between different actors. Still, many interesting patterns emerge from the study, which are likely to be characteristic of large parts of the country.
3. In Andhra Pradesh, the results of IRDP and public works programmes in reaching the poor are particularly bad. (World Bank 1998:42).

REFERENCES

DRDA (1998). *A Note on Developmental Activities in Nalgonda District.* Submitted to the Hon'ble Chief Minister Sri Nara Chandrababu Naidu during his visit to Nalgonda District on 04.12.1998.

NABARD (1996). *Potential Linked Credit Plan—1997-98 to 2001-02 : Krishna District, Andhra Pradesh (with detailed exercise for 1997-98).* Hyderabad : Regional Office, NABARD.

NABARD (1998a). *Potential Linked Credit Plan 1999-2000 : Nalgonda district.* Hyderabad : Regional Office, NABARD.

NABARD (1998b). *District Oriented Monitoring (IRDP): A Study in Krishna District,* Hyderabad : Regional Office, NABARD.

NABARD (1998c). *Study of DWCRA Groups (Nalgonda).* Hyderabad : Regional Office, NABARD

NABARD (1998d). *Role of Informal Credit Delivery Systems (Krishna).* Hyderabad : Regional Office, NABARD

NABARD (1998e). *Banking with the Poor: Financing Self-Help Groups.* Hyderabad : Regional Office, NABARD.

World Bank (1998). *Reducing Poverty in India. Options for More Effective Public Service.* Report 17881-IN. Washington, DC : The World Bank.

3

The Role of NGOs in State-Managed Development

Some Lessons from Nalgonda District

N.L. NARASIMHA REDDY

INTRODUCTION

The development practice in India has special concern for the poor and marginalised sections of the society. This has led to special provisions, resource allocations and delivery mechanisms within the state and the central government development programmes. The State's leading role in the formulation and implementation of development programmes proceeded along with the retention and strengthening of hierarchical structures. As a result, administrators and officials worked to fulfil the requirements of planned programmes/schemes for which they were held responsible, and people's participation had little role to play.

That access and entitlement of earmarked resources for the poor and marginalised served as a constraint in state-managed development is not in dispute. This provided the space for NGOs to empower the poor people so as to participate in the state managed development process. NGOs tread uneasily in the cracks and spaces of the state managed development system. Although, the contribution of NGOs to Indian rural development is very small, it is considered to be effective. One school of development practitioners advocate that the manner in which NGOs seek to supplant the effort of the state as the provider of basic services and development programmes would not only weaken the relationship between the people and the system, but also result in wastage of earmarked resources with more and more non-targetted group cornering such resources. In response, some NGOs have preferred to change the role from that of provider of services to facilitators in enabling the people to access the resources through their own strength. Homo Sapiens falls into this category.

This chapter examines Homo Sapiens' (working in Nalgonda district of Andhra Pradesh) experience in enabling people to command government resource entitlements, which form a large base for development. It views that NGOs should create space for elimination of exploitation in development programmes through collaborative relations, enabling people's participation and self-reliance. This is to complement the work of the government in the light of objectives that the NGO has set for itself.

Development policy of Homo Sapiens has evolved on the basis of following assumptions: (i) local rural development is pursued through local state institutions (both elected and administrative), banking system, non-state institutions, etc.; and (ii) facilitate greater participation and assertion of influence by the poor and socially marginalised in planning and implementation of development programmes. With failure to reach the disadvantaged and remote habitations, the focus of attention is shifting towards micro-level actors (NGOs) and specific forms of community institutions (SHGs, VSS, etc.). Thus, the argument for a potential role for the two institutional categories (namely, government and NGOs) has gained momentum in the early 1990s.

The shift can be seen as a response to a number of factors .First, failure of state-managed development to effectively reach the marginalised and excluded sections of the population. Second, the development resources being processed through different institutions are wasted with wrong-targetting, duplication, diversion, lack of proper utilisation and convergence. Third, developmental activities are target oriented. Fourth, general linking of development with institutional collaboration and networking in terms of empowering the citizen.

THE INTERVENTION STRATEGY OF HOMO SAPIENS

Homo Sapiens began development intervention with child education. In order to become a competent actor in the development process, it undertook scientific needs assessment. On this basis, a programme was evolved to address the tribal needs with the help of resources available within the system; the programme specified a facilitator role for Homo Sapiens.

The project operates in Peddavura mandal of Nalgonda district (Andhra Pradesh). While the area of operation increased from 13 villages in 1996 to 25 villages in 2000, the number of SHGs also increased from 11 to 85 during the same period (Table 3.1). The area comprises of poor agricultural land, a larger part of which has been reclaimed from wasteland that once was a forest. The farmers cultivate a single rain-fed crop. Weak resource position (availability, mobilisation and utilisation), crop failures, seasonal unemployment and lack of alternative employment sources, lack of credit options, and accumulation of debts and poverty made the migration necessary for the tribals.

Table 3.1 : Operational details of the Homo Sapiens

Year	*No. of villages covered*	*No. of clusters*	*No. of SHGs (female groups)*	*Target group (Females)*
1997	13	1	11	Tribal women
1998	13	1	15	Tribal women
1999	20	2	58	Tribal & SC women
2000	25	4	85	Tribal & SC women

Tribals in this area are dependent on middlemen for development programmes. Poor access to local development resources is a major constraint as political favouritism in the disbursement of development work and institutional manipulation to secure local power base are in operation. The issues like resource diversion results in delays and change in priorities, while leakages, personal corruption and bad repayment come in the way of implementation of anti-poverty programmes. The situation, though not different from other areas in the country, demands an effective strategy for tapping available resources and establishing institutional relations. Based on this, Homo Sapiens adopted a strategy "to enable the people to mobilise own resources and to command government resource entitlement with emphasis on eliminating exploitative intermediaries". Towards this objective, the organisation started to depend less on external donors (Table 3.2).

Table 3.2 : Sources of funds mobilised (Rs).

Year	*External Donors*	*Government*	*Total*
1997	232,300 (95.48)	11,000 (4.52)	243,300 (100)
1998	238,020 (13.69)	1,500,000 (86.31)	1,738,020 (100)
1999	437,390 (58.37)	312,000 (41.63)	749,390 (100)

Note : Figures in parentheses indicate percentage to total.

Today, Homo Sapiens operates to enable participation and empowerment of tribals, especially poor in self-help promotion. It has set out to establish organisations of the poor (SHGs), whose primary function is to operate savings and credit activity, whose underlying purpose is to critically collaborate with the government to get benefits from the system. Since Homo Sapiens' experience so far has been linking people with local development resources, this paper analyses government and NGO interface from this angle. Homo Sapiens has four tasks in this process: (i) relations with people; (ii) relations with local government; (iii) interface between people and local government; and (iv) moulding quality of development indirectly. The savings and credit activities provide the basis for establishing the above facets.

Establishing collaborative institutional process and intervening at strategic institutional points towards collective strength is based on specific circumstances, opportunities, individual relations, trust building, mutual reliability, involvement of people and legitimacy of the programme intervention. Whether and how these institutions relate themselves is discussed in the following paragraphs.

THE INTERFACE

Homo Sapiens began efforts towards collaboration at the stage of needs assessment wherein it sought to involve government officials to identify resources (options) availability/gaps *vis-a-vis* needs and attend to grievances presented by the villagers. When Homo Sapiens approached the government officials, there was reluctance to participate in this kind of process. One official stated that this was a smaller constituency and that he had large geographical area to look after.

People were also not prepared to involve as they were used to delivery approaches and were antagonistic towards government machinery. This reflects lack of trust, the roots of which can be traced to a long-list of unaddressed issues (i.e., land rights, basic needs, absence of communication with official machinery and negligence by line departments). Into this environment, the Home Sapiens entered.

Their attempts did not succeed until a "two-day programme between officials and local leadership" was organised. Here, people presented a long list of grievances: forest occupied agricultural lands, private loans, high input agriculture, crop failure, children have no access to schooling, middlemen, etc. From this dialogue process the organisation gained perceptions, limitations, and future strategies. This led to the use of the mechanism of "Dialogue Meetings" at frequent intervals. These meetings also germinated trust among the concerned actors. Out of these meetings emerged an attempt to facilitate the demands for alternative possibilities.

The community approached Homo Sapiens with a long-list of grievances. To reorient people, community 'orientation process' was proposed as a follow up measure. This was directed at delineating the role responsibilities and to differentiate between wants and development needs. In this way, the organisation tried to prepare the people on roles of people, government institutions and Homo Sapiens. Yet, people, preferred to play a passive role on the grounds that in the other NGO project areas people were expected only to receive benefits from NGOs, and they were not expected to mobilise resources from the government.

To overcome this resistance, people were prepared by providing awareness and building their capacity, while officials were constantly consulted. This resulted in rapport building. To graduate this rapport into trust the Homo Sapiens organised direct interaction between people and government machinery. During this phase, a twin-process was adopted, and this had broad based Homo Sapiens' interface with the government: (i) preparing and facilitating people to meet officials directly and represent their grievances; (ii) preparing people for improved participation in all government programmes. But, when an informal assessment took place after one year, the learning was that by encouraging the people to have linkages with the government the organisation had put itself into pressure kind of situation and raised expectations among them that resources will ultimately flow.

With the growth of SHG the need for interface was felt more intently; demand meetings and formation of an apex of SHGs improved the space for participation or SHG members. The argument put forward here is that a more aware community is able to negotiate with the state and share responsibilities. The following methods have been used to facilitate opportunities, services, and anti-poverty programmes :

- Organisation of dialogue meetings with officials on issues by people at regular intervals. This process helped to highlight local issues and to prepare people on official viewpoint and possibilities.
- Village visits and meetings by officials to have first hand information on local situation.
- Preparing people for improved participation in government programmes through information dissemination.
- Feedback to government machinery on local problems, and programmes. Volunteers act as important link in this feedback.
- Demand meetings to address lapses in delivery of local development resources. Demand meetings are intended to enable people to have face-to-face dialogue with officials.
- An apex of SHGs was formed to involve SHG members in decision and actions relating to the interface, and to gain legitimacy.
- Programme and institute specific relation building mechanisms are constantly planned. Officials from the banks, District Rural Development Agency (DRDA) and Modified Area Development Agency (MADA) were involved in group meetings, assessment and resource planning.
- Submission of monthly progress reports on SHGs to all the concerned departments.
- A booklet on district level government programmes related to environmental issues was prepared to disseminate the information. The same was made available for village volunteers. This booklet basically attempted to generate programme database at the village level. The NGO is planning to develop database further at the village level.

To strengthen this process further, a micro-action plan for constituting an area development under the senior district official has been submitted to the district collector. This is intended to improve the institutional collaboration and avoiding duplication. This is yet to materialise.

Perspectives on changing state-society relations

Homo Sapiens' intervention has two favourable impacts; first, that the organisation's activity helped mitigate effects of the prevailing state development process on the poor and disadvantaged; and second, its growing activity enhanced capacities of the poor by institutionalisation of their responses.

Political conditions in Andhra Pradesh

Development governance assumes that state institutions will facilitate greater participation and assertion of influence by the poor and socially marginalised in planning and implementation of development programmes. With failure to reach disadvantageous and remote habitations, there has been a growing recognition of the need to develop and apply appropriate institutional frameworks for development intervention by the state. In recent years there has been growth of participatory community institutions (supported by the state government) with institutionalisation of different responses for meeting diverse needs with the local communities. Substantial expansion of specific forms of community institutions (SHGs, VSS, etc.) are supposed to articulate the demands of the poor and marginalised.

Institutional and human capacity building

The state's focus is, thus, shifting towards developing self-reliant and self-managed community based organisations. Closer scrutiny of self-help groups initiated by the government reveals the obvious limitations with reference to institutional capacity building and main-streaming the poor and marginalised. Thus, for example, in Nalgonda district, a large number of *samabavana* groups (savings and credit groups for women) were formed in 1995-96. A concern expressed was that a large number of women belonged to not-so-poor and better-off communities and their main motive to get into groups was to corner programme benefits, while women from poor and disadvantaged sections were once again left out of the process. Further, the formation raised false expectations due to wrong perspective building by line department which resulted in disintegration or passiveness of a majority of the groups.

In the above context, Homo Sapiens initiated a process in Peddavura mandal in such a way that it would not result in duplicating the government effort. The organisation mobilised women belonging to the poor and disadvantaged groups to form into SHGs, reoriented the existing groups (including those formed by the government) and conducted regular programmes aimed at perspective building and institutional capacitisation. It is to be noted that all those groups formed by the organisation are being enlisted in the mandal records to avoid any discrimination against groups formed by the organisation. This was followed up by submitting monthly status reports to all the concerned departments. In addition constant dialogue and demand meetings between SHG members and officials were organised based on needs. All the above had a positive impact on the interface between SHGs and government institutions and banks.

The intervention of Homo Sapiens enabled the group members to become active participants in group management, information sharing, linkages with the government, MADA and banking institutions. This success resulted in the spread effect to enable more and poorer joining the SHGs in the mandal. This also received a further boost in 1998-99 with DWCRA grants-mela by the government. And now, the organisation has to facilitate the demand system for linking groups with DWCRA grants on the basis of group performance and democratic group assessment process. The apex of SHGs adds strength to the above. Yet, lot more needs to be done in this area.

Micro-institutional points

A discussion on micro-institutional issues becomes essential because the effective utilisation of resources and achievement of desired results will depend on collaborative relations between political, demonstrative and participatory structure. The main focus is, therefore, to locate space for micro-institutional point, i.e., NGOs and participatory structure (for example, SHG) at the grass root level. The experience of Homo Sapiens indicates inseparable relationship between identification of institutional points and expanding the resources at the disposal of the poor.

Since 1997, the organisation has been geared not only to enhance human capital of all poor people, but also help them participate in a range of entitlement related issues such as drinking water for Nagarjunapeta, right on forest occupied lands for Mulathanda inhabitants, involving people in Joint Forest Management, linking *samabavana* members with anti-poverty programmes (MADA and child development opportunities).

Drinking water issue

SHG members resolved the drinking water issue in Nagarjunapeta by making demands on officials from mandal to district levels. First, they met the district collector with the facilitation of the organisation and got the sanction. Then they approached a geologist for the identification of the borewell point. Private rig owners were not interested to go to this village as it is remotely located, and difficult to gain access. After repeated petitions to the district collector and repeated visits to officials at different levels, the villagers protested in front of the collectorate to finally get the programme grounded (Table 3.3). The whole process took more than one year.

Land rights

Mulathanda is located in a forest adjacent to Nagarjuna Sagar. The villagers have been cultivating forest land without any valid legal rights. This has been happening for the last 40 years. The villagers initially came to Nagarjuna Sagar Dam as labourers and settled here. Since then, they had to put up with forest departments and related cases. They got averse to plantation, thinking that the plantation drive would take away their lands. There was resistance from the community to take up joint forest management. In view of this, the NGO initiated a dialogue between district forest officials and villagers. It also organised a series of meetings at the project level and visits to villages by forest officials. During these consultations, people were counselled to form into JFM. While demarcating the area for JFM, the officials excluded cultivation lands of the villagers (Table 3.3). There is also an on-going demand for legal rights. The District collector and revenue officials conducted a survey and the forest department insisted on a joint survey. The joint survey is pending as the concerned departments are not able to locate proper records. But the struggle is on. The only difference is that now they are empowered to fight on their own.

Table 3.3 : Local government programmes

Year	*Name of the programme*	*No. of villages covered*	*Households benefited*	*Total assistance (Rs. in lakhs)*
1997	Drinking water	2	250	3*
1998	JFM	5	800	15.00
1999	DWCRA	9	206	3.12
2000	MADA	1	10	6.8#
	• VSS-SHG Linkages	2	37	0.45
	• Bank-SHG Linkages	10	300	2.40
	• DWCRA	1	16	0.24

Note : * Indicates hand pumps;
Only five units were grounded and the process is on to get other units grounded.

Linkages with anti-poverty programmes

Three banks (i.e., Canara Bank, Andhra Bank and Nagarjuna Grameen Bank) have adopted the area. For the past four years, anti-poverty programmes under MADA could not take off, the reason being bad repayment record in the area. The NGO has, however, facilitated a dialogue meeting between Nagarjuna Grameena Bank Manager and SHGs. As a follow-up, the manager visited SHGs, interacted with SHG members and participated in group meetings. Villagers were counselled to repay the overdues to the bank and re-establish the banking relations. Some of the villagers repaid the dues and availed the crop loans. Subsequently, the linkage with MADA was also facilitated. The manager took innovative steps to link SHG members with MADA loans. All the groups in Nellikal gram panchayat have identified members for the benefits through group consultations. A list prepared by the group members was presented to the officials visiting the group for the beneficiary selection. Consequently, the Bank Manager gave his consent.

At that stage, there was interference by middlemen and political leaders who kept feeding the people with misinformation. Some of them even challenged the women members of SHGs by stating that "we will shave off our moustache if you get the loans". The Mandal officials refused to forward the applications on two counts: first, the number of beneficiaries selected were more than the mandal quota; and second, the activities proposed by the SHG members were not matching with the priorities arrived at the district level. After several consultations by SHG members with mandal officials the applications were forwarded on meeting their costs.

The district administration was against granting sheep units on the ground that the past experience suggested misutilisation of loans in sheep rearing. Homo Sapiens had series of consultations with the officials and requested them to view the proposals of people positively. Finally, the MADA released the cheque to the concerned bank. By that time the Manager got transferred. Immediately, Homo Sapiens had to appraise the process to the new Manager afresh. As part of gaining confidence, once again the NGO organised meetings between SHGs and the Manager. This was followed by dialogue and demand process at various levels. Finally, he started to ground the sheep units (Table 3.3). After grounding five units, he discontinued on the ground that there was an instruction from the district collector not to go ahead with such risky projects. The process of struggle once again began.

This process has three unique aspects : (i) linking anti-poverty programme intended for individual beneficiaries with SHGs could be beneficial for promoting group activity; in fact, two members were grouped for each loan and systems were proposed for group control; (ii) SHG members have not only identified the beneficiaries and activities though group consultations, but also agreed to monitor the entire programme; and (iii) the bank manager gave consent to sanction more units to utilise the unused resources in the other banks in the area after seeing the group dynamics and getting convinced with group cohesion.

Linkages with resource agencies

In addition, the NGO has linked, directly or indirectly, with resource agencies to facilitate integrated development. First, it had direct relationship with M. V. Foundation of Exploring Child Development Opportunities. Altogether, 160 children (school drop outs) were integrated with formal schools and tribal welfare hostels. Second, it linked SHG member households with scientists from Acharya N. G. Ranga Agricultural University for sustainable agriculture, crop-cycle based agriculture extension and village seed banks.

Information on government resources

Perspectives on government resources were generated through dialogue-demand meetings which gave information on benefits, procedures and capacity needed to have entitlement to the benefits. Volunteers will disseminate it further, motivate and prepare people towards active participation. This process has been useful in providing linkages with the resources agencies and programmes possibilities.

CONCLUSIONS

When government officials started to respond positively, people oscillated with delays. Frequent transfers of officials do not allow the interface to settle-down as there is no institutional mechanism. The varied mind-set at different levels of the official machinery has been a concern. Yet, empowered people and their institutional base can give them strength to gain the required space. Only such a change in the interface between government and people can result in a meaningful action-base for right interface.

4

Sanghamithra Service Society and Government Agencies

K. SIVAJI*

INTRODUCTION

Sanghamithra Service Society (hereafter, Sanghamithra) has been working in the western part of Krishna district for the last 13 years in the area of poverty alleviation and empowerment of women. It has had considerable success in the formation of organisations among the target group members for poverty alleviation and empowerment. Over the years, Sanghamithra has laid considerable emphasis on mobilisation of resources from the local government and central government agencies. This chapter discusses the factors contributing to the interface between the target group and government agencies and the strategies that Sanghamithra along with the target group has adopted in facilitating the interface process. It also discusses the problems faced and the impact of the interface on the target groups.

Sanghamithra is a registered NGO. Although the organisation was registered as a society in 1984, it began its rural development works in 1985. In 1999, it was working in 15 villages of

* Thanks are due to Dr. D. Rajasekhar for his comments on an earlier draft of this paper and his generous help in editing it. I also thank Ms. P. Pushpa Rani for her assistance in collecting data from the target group members in three villages.

Kanchikacherla mandal in Krishna district. In addition, it also started a destitute women rehabilitation centre at Telaprolu village of Vungaturu mandal in Krishna district. Sanghamithra also works with 1,210 households in an urban slum in Vijayawada town.

The main area of operation of Sanghamithra is Kanchikacherla mandal where the organisation works with 3,010 members; of them, 95 per cent are women, while the rest are men. Of the total target members, about 50 per cent are *dalits*, the rest belong to minority and economically backward communities. The main activities of the organisation are: (i) Self-help promotion through the formation, strengthening and consolidation of self-help groups; (ii) building the capacity of target group members by conducting various need based training programmes; and (iii) formation and strengthening of the federation of SHGs, and also working with other NGOs. Sanghamithra had been able to form 84 self-help groups by 1998 (Table 4.1). The members in the self-help groups mobilise savings and revolve the same to meet their consumption and short-term production needs. In addition, the target group members also take loans from the organisation to initiate income generating programmes or to strengthen their existing income generation activities.

Table 4.1 : Progress of SHGs in the project area of Sanghamithra

Year	*No. of villages*	*No. of target groups*			*No. of target members*		
		Male	*Female*	*Total*	*Male*	*Female*	*Total*
1996-97	9	—	40	40	—	510	510
1997-98	11	1	72	73	18	907	925
1998	11	1	83	84	18	1,050	1,068

INTERFACE BETWEEN THE TARGET GROUP OF SANGHAMITHRA AND THE GOVERNMENT

Another activity that is pursued by Sanghamithra and its target group is facilitating a linkage with government departments. The importance of this linkage is evident from the data presented in Table 4.2. The information shows that Sanghamithra does not depend on any single agency for undertaking its activities. In 1997-98, Sanghamithra had four sources, i.e., external donors, people, government and Sanghamithra's own sources. While external donors contributed less than 19 per cent of the total resources, the government contributed nearly 36.45 per cent. Secondly, the organisation gives considerable importance to the mobilisation of resources from the people. The target group contributed less than 6 per cent of the total resources during 1997-98 mainly in the form of savings and contributions towards the programme, travel costs, local hospitality, etc. Thirdly, Sanghamithra mobilised over one-third of the total resources from the government. These resources were not exclusively mobilised by Sanghamithra and the people have played a very significant role in obtaining the resources on their own.

Table 4.2 : Resources mobilised during 1997-98

Sources	*Total amount mobilised (in Rs.)*	*Percentage*
Donors	777,210.80	18.73
Sanghamithra Service Society	1,633,299.05	39.36
People	226,627.00	5.46
Government	1,512,890.00	36.45
Total	4,150,026.85	100.00

The interface, according to the organisation, is 'a better relationship between three partners, namely, government, NGOs and their target group'. Interface also implies that both the actors should have capabilities and strengths. When it comes to SHGs, the creditability gained through capacity building programmes is their main strength. Sanghamithra also feels that if the NGO has transparency, accountability, technical know-how and adoption of systematic procedures, then there is good scope for forging better linkages with the government. It should be noted that linkages and/or interface should be viewed in a broader perspective, and should not be confined to that of mere donor and receiver relationship. The linkage process should aim at achieving greater equity in the relationship between the two important actors in rural development.

FACTORS CONTRIBUTING TO INTERFACE

Having defined the interface, let us now discuss the factors that contributed to the interface between Sanghamithra's target group and government agencies.

Sustainability of the programmes and empowerment of the people

Sanghamithra considers that interface with government is very important for achieving the main objective, i.e., achieving people-centred rural development by forming and strengthening sustainable people's organisation. It feels that the interface is needed to sustain the programme initiated for the poor and the marginalised. The needs of the people continuously rise, and it is difficult to meet all their needs with resources mobilised from the donors. In addition, the sustainable poverty alleviation presupposes a change in the conditions and structures that determine decision-making in the allocation of resources by the government. Only when the poor have control over these structures will there be sustainable poverty alleviation. Further, the objective of empowerment of the people also makes it crucial for the NGOs to facilitate the linkages with government agencies.

Role Transformation of NGOs

Sanghamithra's future plan is to make people's organisation sustainable, and transform its own role in such a way that the role of the NGO gradually comes down while that of people's organisation improves. As per the plan, Sanghamithra will function with a small core staff in the future with resources largely mobilised from the government agencies for its own sustainability.

Uncertain donor environment

One of the important factors contributing to improved interface is uncertain donor environment that the organisation has experienced in the last 13 years (Box 4.1). Continued uncertainty in the donor environment influenced the organisation to think of alternative resources with which the programmes could become sustainable. Hence, the organisation gives considerable emphasis to savings and credit programmes which should become an instrument of self-help promotion, where self-reliance, self-management and self-sustainability become very important. The organisation feels that local resource mobilisation plays an important role in achieving this objective.

LEVELS OF INTERFACE

From the inception, Sanghamithra facilitated linkages at two levels: first, direct resource mobilisation by Sanghamithra for its self-reliance, sustainability and ultimate role transformation; and second, facilitating a process by which the SHGs mobilise resources directly from the government for the sustainability of programmes initiated for members. This becomes important for self-help promotion and empowerment of the people. According to the NGO, people must be aware that it is the responsibility of the government to look after the welfare of its citizens, and that it is the right of each person to avail government support for her/his betterment.

Box 4.1: Donor uncertainties faced by Sanghamithra

Sanghamithra initiated its work with child sponsorship programme supported by Action-Aid, an UK based donor agency. The partnership progressed very well until 1989. The donor agency requested Sanghamithra to send a proposal for 200 children. In the meanwhile, the policy of Action-Aid with regard to the organisational aspects of NGOs changed. As per the new policy: (i) the governing board should not consist of relatives; (ii) there should be two staff members of Action -Aid in the governing board of the NGO; (iii) NGOs are not allowed to work with other donors; and (iv) Action-Aid would support only those NGOs who have the capacity to undertake 2,000 children sponsorship. Sanghamithra did not agree with these policy changes, and hence, the partnership came to an end.

Subsequently, the organisation obtained funds from HEKS, a Switzerland based donor agency, for the formation of village level organisations for both men and women. However, these two organisations had to part their ways, as there was change in the policy of HEKS, which emphasised that Sanghamithra should only take up agitations. This was unacceptable to Sanghamithra. The partnership came to an end in 1990.

Sanghamithra, therefore, faced uncertainty for some time and finally obtained funding support from GPC/EZE, a Germany based donor operating in India through Gandhi Peace centre. This partnership came to an end recently as Sanghamithra felt that the donor agency was not really serious about partnership. The donor agency insisted on certain changes in the programme which would go against the overall objective of the organisation.

The NGO along with the target group members mobilised programmes relating to smokeless *chulhas,* housing, dairy development, awareness and training from the state and central governments (Table 4.3).

STRATEGIES ADOPTED

Sanghamithra adopted the following strategies to enable the target group to have strong interface with government agencies. The first and foremost important strategy was to ensure that there was quality stress in the implementation of the programmes sanctioned by the government. Over the years, Sanghamithra realised that creativity, accountability, transparency and people's participation in the programmes go a long way in building a strong and sustainable interface. For instance, when the sanitation programme was sanctioned by the government, the NGO could have implemented the programme by deploying some of its staff members. But, this would not have contributed to people's participation and transparency. Hence, Sanghamithra held detailed discussions with the people, and planning was done in association with them. The target group members formed themselves into purchase committee, monitoring committee, etc., to take control of the entire process of implementation. There were agreements between SHG members and masons, carpenters, etc. This process ensured that people participated in the programme, understood the objectives of the programmes and worked for the successful utilisation of the resources.

Table 4.3 : Mobilisation of resources

Year	*Name of the programme*	*Sources of funding*	*No. of villages*	*No. of benefi-ciaries*	*Total assistance (in Rs.)*
1995-96	Smokeless *Chulhas*	State	13	46	29,144
	National Environment Awareness Campaign (NEAC)	Central	13	4	4,000
	Rural Development, Agricultural Activities, Housing	Donor	16	1,887	804,273
1996-97	Housing	State	1	1,211	17,559,500
	SHG Leaders' Training	State	11	158	55,000
	Dairy	State	1	22	143,000
	Rural Development, Housing	Donor	12	1,787	2,198,845
1997-98	SHG Leaders' Training	State	11	156	1,443
	NEAC	Central	10	67	7,000
	Rural Development	Donor	12	2,136	777,211
1998*	Rural Development, Flood Relief	Donor	12	2,261	394,934

Note : * Data covered up to November 1998.

The second strategy adopted by Sanghamithra was to ensure that they attended all the meetings called by the officials. A widespread practice among the NGOs is that they do not attend the meetings called for by the government officials and approach them only when they need resources. This, in the opinion of Sanghamithra, will not encourage the interface. Wherever and whenever it is possible, the NGO and the target group should participate in the meetings called by the government and should put forward their viewpoints relating to the design and implementation of government programmes, in particular, and rural development, in general. With this strategy, it is possible to correct the mis-conception among government officials that the NGOs exist only for availing the resources from the government. The NGOs and the target group should utilise such meetings to make the point that they can also contribute to the policy-making.

The strategy that worked for Sanghamithra was its attempts to introduce innovations in the sanctioned government programmes. In the experience of Sanghamithra, there is little scope for introducing innovations in the existing government programmes. In spite of it, Sanghamithra made sincere attempts to introduce innovations so that sustainability of the programmes could be ensured. For instance, when the subsidy amount was released to the SHGs, Sanghamithra convinced the people that this amount needed to be repaid to the group in the interest of sustainability. Accordingly, the group members repaid the subsidy amount to the group. With this, the revolving credit fund at the disposal of the group increased and paved way for many more members to utilise the resources. This appealed to the government officials and contributed to further linkages with government agencies.

Sanghamithra organised meetings and discussions between officials at the senior level and target group members. In these meetings, the government officials provided information on procedures relating to the existing programmes while the people expressed their problems, difficulties and constraints. These meetings helped the people and officials to come closer to each other.

At times, Sanghamithra and SHG members agreed to take responsibility to implement certain government programmes although they were not part of their planned programmes. The decision to take part in such meetings was made only when they were certain that such programmes would help the target group directly, and contribute to achieving the overall objective of the organisation. For instance, in the pulse polio programme, the Sanghamithra organised meetings at the village level, provided awareness to the community, identified the children to be given polio drops, prepared a list and made arrangements for some hospitality to the doctors during the health camps.

Sanghamithra gives utmost priority to transparency. The records maintained for the programmes sanctioned are always clear and up-to-date. They are always made available to the concerned officials on request. They also send accounts at periodic intervals to the concerned officials. For a strong and sustainable interface, it is always important to maintain credibility with the government officials. If, for some reason, the organisation is not in a position to take up the programme, it should be stated at the very beginning.

Another strategy that Sanghamithra adopted was to make an impressive presentation of the problem with proper data and information. Whenever target group members approached the government officials, they went with documents highlighting the needs of the people, the methodology adopted in finding out these needs. With this information, the target group members could convince the officials that their needs were genuine and the government should come forward to help them.

Mass representation to the higher-level government officials was taken up whenever there was delay in sanctioning the programme. In 1992, the government agreed to sanction housing programme to the poor in a village. When there was enormous delay in disbursing the funds, people from this and other villages undertook a rally to the Collector to press for the early disbursement of funds.

Another strategy adopted by the NGO was to have linkages with other like-minded NGOs who shared their vision, objectives and understanding. In collaboration with such a group of NGOs the organisation emerged as a nodal agency to implement the water and sanitation programme during 1998-99.

PROBLEMS FACED

Although the above strategies have been adopted by the organisation and SHG members to establish strong interface with the government, there are a number of bottlenecks or problems when it comes to resource mobilisation from the government. These bottlenecks are related to all the relevant actors, namely, NGOs, government and people. Hence, the problems faced by each of these actors have been mentioned below.

Problems *vis-a-vis* NGOs

Sanghamithra feels that there is need to classify NGOs under these categories: (i) Committed, social service and social work minded NGOs; (ii) NGOs promoted by politicians; and, (iii) NGOs promoted by contractors. The first category of NGOs faces a number of problems compared to the second and third categories. In order to get the government programmes sanctioned, the second and third categories of NGOs do not mind bribing the officials. They also keep information to themselves and do not share with others. They have negative attitude towards the first category of NGOs. Such NGOs often misuse the funds received from the government and utilise them for strengthening or setting up their own business. With these problems, the first category of NGOs finds it very difficult to convince the government officials on the potential advantages of NGOs.

Another problem faced by the genuine NGOs is that they are not able to have viable and strong networks. Mutual distrust, jealousy and ideological differences come in the way of the formation of networks. Even if networks come into existence, they mainly work for mobilising resources from the government. As the formation of networks was not process based, a majority of the NGOs in such networks do not have common understanding, objective, vision, belief in democratic systems and transparency. Hence, it becomes very difficult to work towards influencing the policy through lobbying and advocacy. This is one of the major bottlenecks that Sanghamithra faces.

Problems from the people's side

Widespread illiteracy among the target group is one of the major constraints when it comes to establishing linkages with government agencies. As a result, they are not very well aware of different departments, schemes, eligibility and processes. Though Sanghamithra has been making sincere efforts to build the capacity of the people in this regard, widespread illiteracy has become a major constraint.

Motivating the self-help group members to approach the government for resources becomes, at times, difficult given the uncertainty and long duration involved in accessing government programmes. The people are unsure that even if they spend time in accessing government resources through collective action, they may not ultimately get the resources. This comes in the way of motivating the people to approach the government departments for their rights and entitlements.

The target group members have to spend large amounts of money on travel and food when they visit the officials. Given the poverty of the target group members, many of them are not in a position to spend such heavy amounts. On several occasions, the SHG members were reluctant to undertake visits to government office located in a town simply because they would lose one day's wage.

The problems and difficulties associated with government schemes often discourage members to have linkages. The widespread corruption at various levels of the government, confusing and complicated procedures, non-availability of information and role of vested interest are all problems that the target group members face in the linkage process, and find it difficult to tackle them on their own. They also do not have strong organisations and networks among them. This comes in the way of establishing a strong people's forum.

Problems from the Government side

- Government programmes are not properly prepared. This comes in the way of effective implementation.
- The capacity and motivation among lower level officials are very low. In the absence of qualitative training programmes meant for such staff members, they often become obstacles to the interface.
- In the government structure there is no opportunity and/or scope for sharing the views and ideas of NGOs with their higher level officials.
- Often, decisions are communicated orally which leads to confusion and lack of clarity. At times, this also leads to manipulation by the lower level officials.
- Information does not reach the local level staff about various programmes that have been designed by the government at higher levels.
- The government agencies follow target-oriented approach rather than process and objective oriented approaches.

- With regard to the implementation of the programmes, time schedule prepared by the officials themselves is not observed.
- Political interference in the allocation of resources and in the implementation of the government programmes is widespread.
- The government agencies are unable to provide information and objectives in a transparent manner.
- Except in the case of a few officials at the higher levels, the accountability of the officials to the public is near absent.

IMPACT OF INTERFACE ON TARGET GROUPS

As noted earlier, Sanghamithra gives prominence to the capacity building of the target group members in establishing linkages on their own. As a part of these efforts, information on government programmes and procedural formalities is provided to the target group in SHG meetings and meetings organised with government officials. Only when these measures have a positive impact on the target group members will there be a possibility of empowering the people. In order to find out the impact of capacity building measures on the target group, a questionnaire was canvassed among 20 self-help group members in three villages. A distribution of sample members by ownership of landholding and caste reveals that a majority of the sample members were landless, small and marginal farmers belonging to the categories of SC and BC (Table 4.4).

Table 4.4 : Socio-economic status of the sample SHG members

	Size of landholdings (%) by					
Caste groups	*Landless*	*Marginal*	*Small*	*Medium*	*Total*	*Actuals*
Backward Caste	25.0	—	75.0	—	20.0	4
Scheduled Caste	55.0	0	22.2	0	45.0	9
Scheduled Tribe	0	22.2	0	0	5.0	1
Others	50.0	16.7	16.7	16.7	30.0	6
Total	50	15	30	5	100	20

A majority of the sample members had some knowledge regarding the programmes such as housing schemes from SC and ST Corporation, sanitary facilities, DWCRA and house sites programmes.

The proportion of the sample members having knowledge of the other programmes mentioned in Table 4.5 seemed to be less. The sample members stated that they came to know of these programmes in SHG meetings and in training programmes organised by Sanghamithra. A few of the members stated that they came to know of the programmes from government officials. A large proportion of the members who availed government programmes stated that they had productively utilised the programme.

Table 4.5 : Knowledge and utilisation of government programmes

Name of the Programme	*Source of information(%) by*				*Programme*		
	NGO	*SHG*	*GOVT*	*Others**	*Total*	*availed*	*utilised*
Public distribution system	10	25	—	50	85	85	85
SC/ST corporation house scheme	40	10	10	5	65	65	65
Sanitary facility	40	10	10	0	60	70	70
DWCRA	35	20	0	0	55	55	55
Land distribution for house site	25	10	5	0	40	40	40
Cattle/dairy	35	10	0	0	45	30	30
Loans to support rural artisans	40	0	15	0	55	50	50
Programmes relating to OAP, Free education, hostel and electricity	0	10	5	0	15	20	15
Loans (land mortgage, crop and subsidiary)	5	5	0	5	0	10	10

Note: * Others include village leaders.

A majority of the sample members who came to know of government programmes availed them. For this, they needed to initiate follow-up measures such as visits to the government offices and bringing the matter to the leaders of Self-Help Groups and NGO staff. In general, the sample members undertook follow-up measures at the government office or with Self-Help Group members. They also stated that they had to face difficulties in accessing the programmes. These problems were delays in sanctioning the programme, frequent visits, interference by vested interests, etc. Seven, out of 20 sample members, however, stated that they did not face any problem. A majority of the sample members stated that they did not pay bribe to the officials although they were asked for it. Only four sample members said that they paid bribe to the government officials and middlemen.

With regard to the question that whether they would be in a position to independently approach the government in future, 12 out of 20 sample members gave affirmative answers (Table 4.6). Three sample members stated that they needed some assistance while two sample members stated that they would like the NGOs to obtain resources for them.

Table 4.6 : Dependency of the target group members in approaching government officials

Particulars	*No. of sample respondents*	*Percentages*
Dependent on the NGO	2	10
Independent in approach	12	60
Independently in the long run	3	15
Need some assistance or escort	3	15
Total	20	100

CONCLUSION

This chapter notes that the interface process is needed for the NGOs to sustain the development programmes initiated for the poor. The uncertain donor environment makes it particularly important for the NGOs to access the resources from the government. This chapter highlights several strategies that Sanghamithra adopted in mobilising the resources.

5

Government Agencies, NGO and their Target Group

Emerging Challenges on Interface

J. SREENIVASA RAO,
P. PUSHPA RANI & R.R. BIRADAR

INTRODUCTION

Chaitanya Jyothi Welfare Society (CJWS), a registered NGO, is working for the empowerment of women in Nellore district of Andhra Pradesh. The founders of the organisation were initially activists with Marxist and Leninist ideology. They thought that by starting a NGO they could take up those issues which could not be taken up as activists. The issues that interested them were deprivation of rights of women, children and weaker sections, and providing legal awareness. The approach followed was mobilisation of the target group by way of rallies, *dharnas*, etc. Naturally, the NGO concentrated on the protection of rights of women, children and weaker sections in the initial stages, say until 1992.

A shift in the development perspective and approach of the organisation occurred when it participated in the anti-arrack movement that took place in Andhra Pradesh in 1992. CJWS supported women in the villages where it was working, and joined the people in their fight against arrack traders. The participation of CJWS in the movement drew women close to the organisation. The anti-arrack movement became successful when the then government introduced prohibition in the state of Andhra Pradesh.

When the movement was successfully completed, the organisation wanted to know from women what could be done further. The discussions revealed that the women did not have sufficient livelihood options, and that their access to credit, skills and raw materials to improve their livelihood opportunities was limited. The NGO, however, did not want to adopt charity and welfare approach to address these issues. They wanted women to be empowered. The organisation, therefore, decided to shift its focus from protection of human rights to facilitating the implementation of developmental programmes by involving women. Subsequently, there was change in the objectives of the organisation. Now, the main objectives of the NGO are to bring socio-economic empowerment of women, building entrepreneurial abilities among women and campaign against child labour.

Consequently, there was also a change in the activities of the organisation. The following are the main activities of the organisation now: (i) formation and consolidation of SHGs; (ii) enabling women to undertake income generating activities; (iii) starting schools for child labourers; and (iv) undertaking watershed and forest management programmes.

The NGO adopted the SHG approach for this purpose. SHGs involved in savings and credit activities were formed in several villages as an entry point to work with women, address their developmental problems and empower them. In 1998, the NGO was working in 40 villages and formed 110 SHGs for 1,760 women (Table 5.1). The NGO works only with women. The coverage of the NGO in terms of number of villages and groups increased between 1996 and 1998. While the number of villages in which CJWS is working increased from 20 in 1996 to 40 in 1998, the number of groups increased from 37 to 110 during the same period. Thus, the organisation adopted the strategy of covering more number of groups in the same villages from 1997. Consequently, the number of members covered by the NGO also increased (Table 5.1).

In addition, the organisation started a child labour school in one of the target villages with funds received from the National Child Labour Project (NCLP). In order to carry out these activities the organisation has 14 field level workers and 4 staff in the administration. Five persons work in the child labour school started by the NGO.

Table 5.1 : The coverage details of CJWS

Year	*Number of villages*	*Number of target groups*	*Total group members*
1996	20	37	592
1997	40	100	1,600
1998	40	110	1,760

Interface with government agencies

One of the objectives of the organisation from the inception was to work with government agencies, and enable the target group to mobilise resources from the system itself. Accordingly, the SHGs formed in the initial stages mainly emerged from out of the DWCRA groups promoted by the government. A rapid expansion in the target area of the NGO, and the objectives of campaigns against child labour and working for sustainable agriculture influenced the NGO to go in for local resource mobilisation.

An examination of data on funds received from government agencies and donor organisations shows that the organisation has been placing considerable emphasis on local resource mobilisation (Table 5.2). The total amount of resources mobilised from both government and donor agencies for three years (1996-98) was Rs. 38.11 lakhs. Of this amount, nearly 70 per cent was mobilised from the state and central governments, while about 30 per cent of the amount was mobilised from donor agencies. This pattern roughly remained the same in all the years except that the contribution of donor agencies was relatively more in 1997 as the organisation received revolving credit fund to initiate income generating activities in that year. During the period 1996-98, the contribution of state and central governments was over 50 per cent. The organisation places roughly equal emphasis on central and state government programmes.

The NGO feels that the following factors contributed to the mobilisation of a larger proportion of resources from state and central governments:

Table 5.2 : Distribution of funding by source (in Rs.)

Year	*State*	*Central*	*Donor*	*Total*
1996	504,000	547,500	300,000	1,351,500
	(37.29)	(40.50)	(22.30)	(100)
1997	544,000	350,000	700,000	1,594,000
	(34.13)	(21.96)	(43.91)	(100)
1998	264,000	424,000	178,000	866,000
	(30.48)	(48.96)	(20.55)	(100)

Note: Figures in parenthesis indicate percentage to total.

- The first important factor is donor uncertainty. When partnership with GTZ/SHF was entered into in 1996, CJWS understood that the main objective of the donor agency was to provide revolving credit funds to enable the target group to undertake income generating activities. The organisation came to realise that the main objective of the organisation was only providing inputs for capacity building.
- Second factor is that if a donor agency suddenly stops funding, this may cause damage to the programme. Hence, CJWS realised that greater reliance on local resource mobilisation was crucial.
- For NGO survival and sustainability of the programme, they need to have linkages with the government.

Meaning of interface

According to the organisation, there is need for critical interface with the government. This implies a process that would result in balanced understanding with the government. The NGOs need to criticise the government if its policies are defective. At the same time, they need to appreciate and encourage the government, if its programmes are functional and pro-poor.

The perception of the organisation is that the purpose of linkages should be to enable the people to gain strength in the linkage process. The people need to be empowered if the linkage process is to become strong and sustainable. It is people's right to utilise the government resources. They should have a dominant say in decision-making regarding the design, implementation and monitoring of the programmes of government.

Establishing linkages

The NGO seeks to establish linkages with government agencies at various levels. Some of the programmes which are currently being implemented are as follows:

- CJWS started Self-Help Groups, which are funded by the state government under DWCRA scheme. The members in these groups undertake savings and credit activities on regular basis. In the group meetings, awareness is provided on various government programmes. As a result, the group members have availed various programmes from the government. In 1996, 600 members in 14 groups obtained revolving credit fund to the tune of Rs. 2.44 lakhs under the DWCRA scheme. In 1997, another 592 women in 20 groups availed Rs. 2.44 lakhs from DWCRA (Table 5.3). In 1998 also, some more groups benefited from the scheme. By enabling the target group to obtain the resources from DWCRA, the organisation has been able to fulfil the objective of providing capital to initiate income generating activities for women members.
- The second major programme obtained from the government was from National Child Labour Project. In 1996, a child labour school was established for 50 children belonging to four villages located in the project area of CJWS. The organisation receives Rs. 1.90 lakhs from the central government every year to run the school (Table 5.3). Under this four-year programme, school drop-outs are provided with educational facilities and are motivated to join the regular schools again. In addition, vocational training in tailoring is also provided. By mobilising resources for the school from the central government, the organisation has been able to fulfil its objective of working towards eradication of child labour. Funds have also been mobilised to organise campaigns against child labour (Table 5.3).
- Third important activity has been setting up of a training centre in palm leaf basket making and cloth weaving with financial support from NABARD. Nearly 25 women have been provided with training for six months. With this activity

the organisation has been able to fulfil the objective of building the skills of the target group members.

- CAPART sanctioned a sanitation programme in 1997. The total budget for this programme was Rs. 1.61 lakhs (Table 5.3). About 80 low cost latrines were constructed for the target group members in the project area of CJWS.
- In addition, resources have also been mobilised from TRYSEM programme for skill building, CMEY programme for group based income generating activities and "Back To School" programme for campaigns against child labour (Table 5.3).

The foregoing discussion suggests that the NGO has been able to mobilise resources from a variety of government programmes to fulfil the objectives that it has set for itself.

Table 5.3 : Mobilisation of resources

Year	*Programmes*	*Sources of funding*	*No. of villages*	*No. of benefi-ciaries*	*Total quantum of assistance (in Rs.)*
1996	DWCRA	State	14	600	244,000
	TRYSEM	State	4	25	260,000
	NCLP	Central	4	50	190,000
	Child Right	Central	4	75	20,000
	Cycles	Central	10	75	337,500
1997	CMEY	State	3	25	100,000
	DWCRA	State	20	592	244,000
	TRYSEM	State	1	40	200,000
	NCLP	Central	4	50	190,000
	CAPART	Central	4	80	160,000
1998	DWCRA	State	40	1,200	250,000
	Back to School	State	1	50	14,000
	NCLP	Central	4	50	190,000
	CAPART	Central	2	80	160,000
	NABARD	Central	1	25	74,000
	IGP	Donor	14	300	178,000

Strategies Adopted

The following are the strategies adopted by the NGO to mobilise resources from the government.

- The NGO has adopted the strategy of maintaining continuous rapport with the concerned officials in the local government by having periodic meetings with them, appraising the activities and programmes of the organisation to them.
- The NGO has impressed the local government officials with its sincerity and capability. The activities that they have taken up from the government such as palm leaf training and, child labour school were implemented very well and the results were achieved. This has had positive impact on the government officials.
- The NGO is successful in enabling the target group members to participate in the village development activities, the women members of SHGs came forward on their own and requested the concerned officials to provide an opportunity to women to participate in road construction under Janmabhoomi programme. When the officials were reluctant to sanction the road construction work to SHG members, they argued their case with the MLA and the Collector, and got the work sanctioned. They have successfully completed the task and impressed all the officials concerned.
- Helping the government in certain programmes. The NGO has been running a training centre on handicrafts and has conducted many workshops for the rural youth. This enabled the organisation to have good rapport with the government officials.

Problems faced in establishing linkages with the government

In establishing linkages with the government agencies the organisation faced the following difficulties and constraints :

- Most of the officials are not positive in their thinking and attitude towards NGOs. Only a few of them give full co-operation.
- The rapport built with officials is often lost due to their frequent transfers. Whenever a new government official

comes to the district, the process of building rapport has to start afresh, and the organisation has to spend considerable time and energy on this.

- The concerned officials often do not have much awareness of the programmes and, hence, do not provide clarity regarding the procedural formalities. This causes enormous delays.
- Cooperation and coordination among government agencies are essential for the successful implementation of development programmes. Often, lack of such cooperation and coordination result in enormous delay. For instance, in the case of a training centre for palm leaf producers, although the organisation established rapport with the NABARD office, lack of coordination between the bank and NABARD resulted in an enormous delay in sanctioning the programme.
- The funds are not released on time. This poses many problems to resource-scarce NGO like CJWS. In the case of CAPART programme, funds were released a year after sanctioning of the programme. In the meantime, the organisation had to spend money received for other programmes.
- There is mutual distrust between the government agencies and NGOs. The government officials do not recognise and acknowledge the NGO efforts in rural development and poverty alleviation. The treatment of some of the officials towards NGOs is not encouraging. This comes in the way of strong interface with the agencies manned by such officials.
- Widespread corruption among government officials is yet another major problem.

Impact of interface on the target group

As noted earlier, the organisation provides awareness on various government schemes to the target group members in SHG meetings, and also hold dialogue meetings with local elected leaders and government officials. The organisation also seeks to build their capacity in approaching and accessing resources from the government. In order to understand the impact of these measures on the target group, a questionnaire was canvassed among 16 members of Self-Help Groups. Most of these members were landless (50 per cent) and small farmers (31.25 per cent). Regarding the caste background, about one-third belonged to backward castes, while 50 per cent were Muslims.

A majority of the sample members were aware of the DWCRA scheme and the provision of bank loans for livestock and agriculture (Table 5.4). Three out of 16 sample members were aware of the programmes such as old-age pension, sanitary facilities, hostel facilities, loans for children's education, family planning, etc. Thus, a large proportion of the sample members were not aware of various programmes initiated by the government except DWCRA programme. This is to be understood in the context that most of the sample members were part of DWCRA groups, and hence, interaction with officials from DRDA was better as compared to the other line departments.

The sample members stated that they came to know of these programmes in the meetings of SHGs and from NGO staff and through dialogue meetings. The proportion of members availing and utilising the programmes has been higher in the case of DWCRA and loans to agriculture, livestock, etc., as compared to loans to support artisans and programmes relating to sanitary, old age pension and free education. This has been mainly due to the group approach followed in the case of DWCRA, and individual approach followed in the case of other programmes. The case studies of 16 members reveal that, in the case of group activities, 5-6 members along with the NGO staff approached the officials, and had continuous follow up. This resulted in good response on the part of officials, and speedy clearance of the application. The incidence of corruption was also less. On the other hand, in the case of individual oriented programmes, the sample faced difficulties such as inordinate delay in sanctioning of the programmes, corruption and inability to follow up with the officials. For instance, a thirty-five year old widow had to wait for over six months to even get a response to what happened to her application for widow pension. She could not follow up as she was the only bread-earner in the household. The disbursal of pension amount is also not continuous, and the amount for 3-6 months is given at a time.

Table 5.4 : Knowledge and utilisation of government programmes

Name of the programmes	*Source of Information (%)*					*Percentage of members*		
	NGO	*SHG*	*Govern-ment*	*Others**	*Total*	*Aware of the programmes*	*Availing the programmes*	*Utilising the programmes*
DWCRA	25	25	12.5	12.5	75	75	68.75	68.75
Loans to support rural artisans	12.5	6.12	6.25	6.25	31.25	31.25	25	25
Programmes relating to sanitary facilities, OAP, free education & hostel	18.75	25	6.25	18.75	68.75	75	43.75	43.75
Loans for agriculture, livestock and under CMEY	37.5	18.75	0	37.5	93.75	100	56.25	56.25

Note : * Include the village leaders.

Notwithstanding the difficulties faced in accessing the resources, most of the sample members reported that the resources helped them to have increased income (Table 5.5). In the case of IRDP loans for sheep rearing, the sanctioned amount was as much as Rs. 21,000 and with this, 15-20 sheep could be bought. By utilising insurance and veterinary facilities, they could also have income security.

Table 5.5 : Impact of the accessed programme

Particulars	*Total No. of sample members*	*Percentage*
Increased income	8	50.0
Income & employment	2	12.5
Resulted in a shelter for living	2	12.5
Community development became possible	2	12.5
No increase in income and expenditure	2	12.5
Total	16	100

Three out of 16 sample members stated that they were now independent in approaching the government officials, while four sample members stated that they were dependent on the NGO for the time being and could function independently in the long-run (Table 5.6). About half the sample members stated that they were dependent on the NGO and SHGs. This suggests that the target group members were yet to become completely independent in approaching the government officials. To some extent, this was due to the inability to strike a balance between capacity building and mobilisation of resources so that the target group could improve their livelihood options. At times, in order to fulfil the expectations of the target group, the NGO had to compromise with the process.

On some other occasion, since the resources were to be obtained in a short span of time, the NGO staff played an important role in obtaining the same.

Table 5.6 : Dependency of the target group members in approaching government officials

Particulars	*Total No. of sample members*	*Percentage*
Dependent on the NGO	3	18.75
Independent approach	4	25.00
Dependent only for the time-being and can function independently in the long run	4	25.00
Dependent on SHGs	2	12.50
Not available	3	18.75
Total	16	100

CONCLUSION

The foregoing discussion suggests that the organisation has succeeded in mobilising resources from the central and state governments. Such mobilisation of resources has proceeded in correspondence with the objectives that the organisation has set for itself. However, the organisation needs to spend considerable time and efforts in building the capacity of the target groups so that they can independently approach and access the resources.

6

Government Agencies and GRAM

Evolution of Strategies that would Work

N. SAMSON

INTRODUCTION

GRAM is a NGO working for rural development in Nizamabad and Adilabad districts of Andhra Pradesh. In 1980, two active members began a set of activities in five villages with funding from the community and external donors. In the last 20 years, the organisation grew and began to undertake many activities in a large number of villages. This chapter documents the 20 years of experience in the promotion of Community Based Organisations (CBOs) formed mainly by *dalits*, women and disabled to influence the policy which affected their lives, interface with government departments and mobilisation of resources from the government. In order to establish interface, the empowerment of the vulnerable groups comprising *dalits*, women and disabled has become an essential component of the organisation.

The major objectives of the organisation are to educate and organise the weaker sections of society towards self empowerment in social, economic and cultural spheres with special focus on issues relating to *dalits*, women and disabled and to promote sustainable organisations in the above spheres of focus which can be owned and managed by the members themselves.

The NGO has initiated the following activities to fulfil its objectives: formation of community organisations of men and women *(sanghas)* and federate them at various levels in the project area; formation of thrift groups for men and women and establish linkages with commercial banks under NABARD's programme as Bank-SHG linkage; activities aimed at skill/capacity building of the community and community based rehabilitation of the disabled; and establishing linkages with the government and enabling people's institution to access the resources.

The NGO has been operating in 416 villages spread over 14 mandals in two districts. The organisation has human resource strength of 134 full-time employees and 3,226 village level volunteers. The poor *dalits* and disabled men and women are the target group members, for whom the organisations were formed. So far, the NGO has formed 1,608 SHGs for women and 491 SHGs for men, comprising of 22,458 female and 6,685 male members. Further, it has promoted and facilitated networking of 216 men and 376 women *sanghas* into three area level federations in the project area.

Interface with the government

The time and experience in NGO sector taught us two distinct development paradigms; the promoters of one group of NGOs hail from (relatively) better off social, economic and political heritage, and the other belong to the oppressed sections of the society. The former enjoys a status (fulfils "enabling" pointers) with formal institutions, do not find it imperative to initiate/contribute/ participate in the essential social change process seriously with regard to the vast majority of oppressed sections of the society, and forms part of the most favoured organisations. The latter mostly dependent on external funding that is not subjective to but sensitive to local social, economic and political conditions, do not find such favourable status as in the case of the former. Often such organisations in their struggle for socio-economic justice irritate the powers that be. At the same time, they are quite harmonious in their thought and development process. Hence, they are co-opted to implement development programmes, which often proves to be negative to the organisational development of such NGOs. GRAM places itself in this category of organisations. Yet, at the same time, it also works with the other category of organisations, whenever and wherever it is strategically important.

In the context of lack of a clear political will, the motive to involve NGOs by government institutions appears to be for two major reasons. First, NGOs are less expensive or "cost effective" as they depend on external funding sources; and secondly, the conditions stipulated by bilateral agencies for NGO's participation. The threatening control mechanisms vested in the government to marginalise non participating NGOs is also an inducing factor for the NGO to have interface with the government

Three special schools for child labourers are being run by GRAM with Central Government assistance through the district administration. Similarly, it has handled 100 Non-Formal Education (NFE) centres through the same district administration's control. In case of child labour schools funds were released after much delay. In case of NFE centres, GRAM was forced to withdraw from the programme after three years of implementation as the allotted funds were not released to pay to the village instructors. At the same time the NFE centres handled by the department received all the arrears. Both child labour schools and NFE centres are operated through two separate registered societies under the chairmanship of the district collector and manned by the departmental staff on deputation. In traditional parlance, effecting payments to government run centres and not paying to NGO run centres would force a negative view against NGOs (as if the whole exercise of involving NGOs is to project them as inefficient). This experience has reduced GRAM's role into a middleman between the NFE instructors and the government. The NFE instructors have been threatening to go on agitation if arrears are not paid to them. One of the reasons for delay in the settlement of arrears is the transfer of concerned officers and the successors always say that they have to read and understand the files and procedures. It appears that the cooperation is not between institution to institution but person to person in the interface process.

In collaboration with Andhra Pradesh Dairy Development Co-operative Federation, GRAM has been promoting 20 women dairy co-operatives in Nizamabad district. Under this programme, all other development departments should have made efforts to converge their resources for the successful implementation of the programme; but this did not happen. NGOs were invited to participate because of their rapport with the people and were expected to motivate them to effectively use the benefits offered by the government departments. The slow pace in the implementation of the dairy programme is attributed to NGO inefficiency rather than to lack of interdepartmental coordination.

Once, at the request of the State Government, GRAM submitted a proposal to run a Primary Health Centre (PHC) for three years and hand over the same to the people. GRAM never received any acknowledgement from the government about their decision. Interestingly, it learnt through the media that the state cabinet deferred the decision to hand over the PHCs to NGOs. Another project in collaboration with government under process was the establishment and management of a carcass utilisation-cum-improved leather tanning project. GRAM made its commitment to provide Rs. 5 lakhs to each of the above projects as part of its stake and received donor commitments. However, both remained as non-starters. GRAM conducted TRYSEM training to voluntary veterinary workers and light motor vehicle drivers for which financial assistance was inadequate. The financial assistance was also reimbursed after lot of avoidable delays by the concerned departments.

NGOs were often engaged by government departments in programmes of intangible benefits such as NFE. Hence, NGOs could not muster popular support for such programmes and became vulnerable to criticism. All these negative experiences did not erode GRAM's belief in cooperation; in fact, they reinforced its belief to find alternatives to co-operate with CBOs.

In the context of GO/NGO co-operation enumerated above, it should be noted that GRAM's strength to find alternatives comes from:

- its role as promoter of a mass organisation;
- its reliance on external funding that is not subjective to but sensitive to the local socio-economic and political conditions;
- its neutrality to party politics; and
- its use value in the implementation of government programmes particularly in the most backward regions hit by political violence.

Strategies adopted

It is important to recognise that strategies can only emerge out of a long term perspective of a NGO that forms core instrument for day-to-day operational strategies. GO-NGO co-operation invariably gives a middlemen role to the NGOs. It is very difficult to wriggle out from such role without creating appropriate alternative. In the case of GRAM, the major strategy was to evolve a sustainable people's initiative through Community Based Organisations network. GRAM tried to play a supportive role to the CBOs so that they could effectively use the opportunities and resources from the government.

The interface with the government is to be understood as means of empowering the poor. Poverty is a structural issue that can be resolved by NGOs alone. Being dependent on external support, NGOs are in less favourable situation to become sustainable organisations. They should, therefore, become tools for promotion of CBOs who will have the power to deal with structural issues of poverty. Simultaneous consolidation and expansion of numerical strength of the target groups is an agenda of the CBO networks—not GRAM's direct agenda. Government and banks have recognised SHGs as core development institutions in rural areas. Facilitation of SHGs into MACS (Mutually Aided Cooperative Societies) at mandal level, federation at district level and further facilitation of a network at state level would cause a strategic alliance between CBOs, GOs and institutions that address the issue of poverty.

There is need to move from conflicts to convergence, and SHG movement provides an opportunity in this. In the past, most of the government programmes were pursued as stand alones. Since SHGs have become core development institutions, the dividend to NGOs comes in the form of DWCRA assistance to SHGs promoted by them. This has had a positive impact on the quality of SHGs promoted by the government. Subsequently, this has had a positive impact on the entire SHG movement in the state. In this programme, certain amount of mutual co-operation is taking place (as strategic partnership) among government, NGOs and CBOs. Thus, SHGs have now become nucleus for convergence of services by all other institutions. For instance, promotion of a *SHG* member as gram panchayat leader has now become as much progressive step to government as it is to CBOs and NGOs.

The interface between government and CBO is far more important. Facilitating GO-CBO interface is a graduation for GRAM; further its sub-ordination role to the process of CBO network is mutually empowering. Today, the CBOs are directly representing their interests while GRAM provides only secretarial services to them. This has made GRAM to be accountable to the CBOs and also to the government. GRAM has made it a policy to give less publicity to its own activities and more publicity to CBO activities. GRAM has also made it a policy that it will promote leaders from among the CBOs rather than itself taking the leadership role. A visible austere measure to reinforce such policy has been taken that no GRAM representative accepts dignitary status in public meetings in preference to CBO leadership promotion. Now it is the CBO leaders and officials who grace all the public meetings.

GRAM acknowledges the role of government and other institutions in the success of the CBO movement. For instance, by meeting the costs on promotion and training of SHGs, GRAM used to claim ownership over CBOs. Now training needs are partly met by NABARD. Revolving fund and subsidies are being provided by government, while commercial banks are lending to the SHGs. It has been a mutually rewarding experience for all the partners to collaborate in this. Now all the partners claim ownership of SHGs.

So far most of the literacy programmes were pursued in isolation rather than addressing the functional needs of the people in their development process. To improve self-management capacities of the CBOs, particularly with regard to SHG records maintenance, over-emphasising on adult literacy and non-formal education to CBO leaders has been given up and a more pragmatic approach of preparing part-time village level professionals has been taken up. However, the need for literacy does not cease with the training of village volunteers. GRAM has been trying to create an effective linkage between NABARD and CBOs to negotiate for affirmative credit to earn operational costs. In turn, NABARD expects minimum functional literacy skills from CBO leadership as an indicator to prove that they have the minimum skills to manage their own affairs. GRAM has not given up literacy but rather pursuing it from a different functional angle. Today the analogy used by some illiterate CBO leaders is very non-conventional and interesting. For instance, Sathyagangu, forty-year old illiterate *dalit* woman president of MACS from Nandipet mandal says, “we should not just learn to read the destination of a bus but how to rule ourselves”. It is hoped that gradually the CBOs take the NFE centres and manage proper utilisation of the resources.

GRAM aims to enable CBOs to become sustainable. The CBOs are able to recruit and pay for the village level staff. This has allowed GRAM to send its staff to accompany the CBOs in their expansion plans. Now five workers are looking after one mandal (20 to 30 villages). It has been planned that, from 2003, one worker will serve one mandal level CEO. Such understanding with CBOs would lead to, as GRAM witnesses, a simultaneous increase in the coverage of villages.

Achieving operational self-sufficiency by CBOs is the first step before attaining financial self-sufficiency. The process includes continuous interface between CBOs, government, banks, and other similar networks to influence the policy for affirmative action. For instance, availability of credit alone does not ensure credit absorption. Without adequate infrastructure development, the poor cannot participate in economic competition. The role of government is primarily to create such infrastructure so that CBOs can work better.

CBOs conceive that their strength lies in broad basing of their network. Often NGO boundaries hinder CEO networking. Since CBOs have now started to network with similar institution elsewhere and empower their geographical area, NGO networking will become an incidental process. GRAM has facilitated two such network meetings between NGOs and CBOs in Telangana and Andhra regions. Interface between PRIs and CBOs have been facilitated as a means and strategy to augment CEO participation in local democratic institutions. GRAM maintains political neutrality in so far as CEO's own loyalties are concerned. The object of self-empowerment is most important and diversity a great asset for the CBOs to find more opportunities of participation and leadership. In order to achieve the desired role transformation between GRAM and the emerging CBOs, GRAM has ceased its self-expansion plans and has begun to subordinate itself to the CEO federation by playing a secretarial role. The federation would in turn evolve its own business and strategic expansion plans.

GRAM uses cultural medium as extensively as possible for education/organisation and communication.

Ijjat, a colloquial Urdu term for self-respect is the title of the monthly newsletter of the *Sanghas*. This has been initiated by GRAM to highlight their success stories. It is expected that the federation will take over the running of the newsletter. It is also a strategy to harness the interest and understanding of the emerging alternative leadership of CBOs.

Promotion and networking of CBOs is both an objective and means for sustained resource mobilisation and capacity building. If that is what the development partners are looking for, a close look into the process in a participatory manner would be mutually rewarding to identify more pertinent issues and processes.

Some outstanding issues

- The government's offers, while being loaded with procedures, expects collaboration with NGOs through the same departments whose effectiveness is reputed to be very low. Mere shifting of implementation responsibilities to NGOs will not serve the purpose. It should rather be supported by alternative procedures with the same seriousness shown for industrial/market development through single window approach under liberalisation drive.
- Bilateral aid stipulations seem to be the prime mover for seeking NGO involvement rather than an objective political will. This often adversely affects the quality of interface process.
- The new trend is that government starts separate registered societies for implementing different programmes. Though they seem to give non-governmental look, for all practical purposes, they remain pure government organisations in their functioning and effectiveness.
- It is not all that excellent with NGOs either. The NGO efforts though focused at grass roots, are not effectively networked to put up a concerted effort to create macro relevance. GRAM is not an exception in this realm of NGOs.
- NGO involvement with government programmes should be a strategy—not necessarily a means of NGO self-sufficiency. NGOs alone cannot change public policy. In fact, the enhanced people's participation in all the democratic institutions will contribute to pro-poor policy development

(NGO self sufficiency—an outcome of new market-oriented economic trend—may perhaps be realised as an incidental development to the promotion and consolidation of CBO institutions). Some NGO-cum-business companies have already turned their focus to cater to the people with more credit absorption capacity with the help of low cost funds to earn profits for their own sustainability and this would undermine the interests of the target groups on whose name the low cost funds were mobilised. Poverty is relative! Well it is ridiculous to compare Bill Clinton with Bill Gates to determine who is poor. Obviously some better off NGO-cum-businessmen seem to have been surviving on this logic to extract capital needed to run their own self-sustainable business. This will undermine the cause of CBOs, which will not obviously have the sophistication, management and manoeuvring skills of NGO-cum-business companies.

7

Interface between Government, NGO and Target Group Members

Experiences of Social Action for Needy People

K. JOJI & P. PUSHPA RANI

INTRODUCTION

Social Action for Needy People (SANP)[1] is a registered NGO founded by a group of social workers. The main concerns of the organisation are: upliftment of weaker sections, Scheduled Castes (SCs), Scheduled Tribes (STs), Backward Castes (BCs) and marginalised groups such as women. The basic objectives of the SANP were, to begin with, mobilisation of poor *dalits*, and bring solidarity and empower them. The organisation has been working in the interior and most backward villages of Doma Mandal of Ranga Reddy District in Andhra Pradesh. The organisation took a very deliberate decision to work in the remote villages where development services had not reached the poor. The people residing in these villages are mainly SCs, STs, and BCs. Most of them are landless agricultural labourers, bonded labourers, rural artisans and small and marginal farmers.

SANP mainly concentrated on the empowerment of *dalit* women, promoting leadership qualities among them, and wiping out the bonded labour. The specific objectives of the organisation now are to: (i) develop self-reliance among the target group members (*dalits*); (ii) provide economic inputs and other facilities as an enabling environment to undertake income generating programmes by the target group; (iii) tap resources from government for the benefit of the poor and needy, and provide quality support to the target group in this regard; (iv) disseminate knowledge through skill development; and, (v) empower *dalits* through community organisation.

The approach followed by the organisation is to form *sanghas* for both men and women. The male groups are called *Bida Aikya Sangham* (Association of the poor), while women are organised as SHGs. The organisation has also formed Maa Mahila Federation for women.

The NGO is working in 50 villages in Doma mandal where it had formed 271 SHGs by 1998. The coverage of the organisation (in terms of number of villages, number of groups and members) increased in the recent years. Significantly, while the male groups increased at a low rate, the female groups increased at a rapid rate (Table 7.1). So much so that the emphasis is almost only on women from 1998 onwards. Secondly, the average size of the male groups is big, while that of female groups is small.

Table 7.1: Progress in the formation of SHGs

	Number	*Number of groups*			*Total target group members*		
Year	*of villages*	*Male*	*Female*	*Total*	*Male*	*Female*	*Total*
1994	11	11	35	46	385	525	910
1995	15	15	50	65	525	750	1,275
1996	20	20	75	95	700	1,350	2,050
1997	21	21	75	96	800	1,400	2,200
1998	50	21	250	271	840	4,000	4,840

Activities of the Organisation

The major activities of the organisation are : (i) promotion of literacy; (ii) conducting animation programmes; (iii) promotion of thrift and credit to bring about a change in the socio-economic status of the target group; and (iv) implementation of desilting and land reclamation (cultivation) programmes. In addition, SANP has undertaken the activity of construction of check-dams to improve irrigation facilities with the help of Water-Aid programme. Another major activity is to tap resources from the local and central government departments.

To undertake all these development activities, the NGO is supported by staff at central and field offices. It has a director, an accountant and a computer operator at the central office at Hyderabad, while there are 8 animators (5 men and 3 women), two security guards and two drivers at the field office.

Interface with government agencies

SANP has been giving importance to interface with the government by involving its target group members. In its opinion, interface refers to interaction between the government and NGOs to facilitate the process towards the utilisation of existing resources within the government. This requires better understanding between the NGOs and the government. The linkage process needs cooperation and coordination between the NGO and the government to bring about convergence in their views.

The organisation feels that the interface is needed to: (i) tap the government resources for the development of the poor; and, (ii) make productive use of the funds available within the government. It is also of the opinion that the resources should directly go to the poor rather than to the organisation.

Keeping these points in view, the organisation has been mobilising resources since the mid 1990s. Table 7.2 shows that the organisation mobilised over 45 per cent of the resources spent on development from central and state governments. Although the proportion of resources mobilised from the government agencies declined to less than five per cent in 1997, SANP still places considerable emphasis on mobilisation of resources from the government. The questions that can be posed here are: what factors contributed to the mobilisation of resources from the government?

Table 7.2 : Quantum of funds mobilised

(in Rupees)

Year	*State*	*Central*	*Donor*	*Total*
1995	255,000 (43.52)	5,000 (0.85)	325,988 (55.63)	585,988 (100)
1996	249,000 (16.99)	5,000 (0.34)	1,211,653 (82.67)	1,465,653 (100)
1997	123,069 (4.28)	5,000 (0.17)	2,747,679 (95.55)	2,875,748 (100)

Note: Figures in parentheses represent percentages.

Mobilisation of external funds

In the beginning, SANP mobilised funds from the target and non-target groups in the form of donations to maintain the NGO. Later, a Dutch donor agency (NOVIB) came forward to support the organisation. Under the New Partners' Funding programme of NOVIB, the organisation obtained funding for a period of three years. At the end of three years, NOVIB stopped funding for a year. During this one-year period, SANP took up several other programmes and continued its work. The sincerity, transparency and excellent performance of SANP, in the absence of NOVIB funding, once again made NOVIB to continue its funding for a period of three years. As on today, the organisation does not have any problem with the donor agency. Though, at times, there are unwarranted delays in donor funding, SANP requires donor support to scale up its activities and to eventually make the programme sustainable in the long run.

Problems faced in establishing linkages with the government

SANP does not recognise the need for direct collaboration with the government for mobilising resources for its programmes. It is also critical of the political and corrupt forces that often hinder development efforts (Boxes 7.1 and 7.2). Further, the government officials do not extend much cooperation and there is lack of openness in them. According to SANP, if the bribe is given, the government officials grant a programme or else they do not sanction the programme on some pretext. Due to this reason, SANP is having limitations towards government programmes and not readily accepting. If corruption was not a hindrance, the organisation would have mobilised more funds.

Box 7.1: Corruption in the allocation of watershed programmes
The local government, on its own, wanted to sanction a watershed programme with an outlay of Rs. 5 crores to SANP. After initial discussion, it became evident to SANP that the officials concerned were expecting a cut from the organisation. SANP also realised that there were many procedural difficulties, which would have made the programme implementation very difficult. If SANP had agreed to undertake this programme despite these problems, it would have amounted to being co-opted into the programme. Hence, the organisation refused the programme rather than being co-opted. The organisation has also faced similar problems with the CAPART.

Box 7.2 : Problems in accessing the centrally sponsored government programmes
SANP has implemented a few Central government programmes. Based on its experience, the organisation feels that the following are important problems associated with the Central government programmes: first, the organisation could not obtain accurate information from the concerned departments regarding the procedure for submitting the applications; second, the duration of time at the disposal of the organisation was short for sending an application; third, there was no communication from the government department despite the follow-up by the organisation; fourth, unwillingness on the part of the departments to send communication about the sanction of the programme made SANP to feel that they would have to pay bribes to obtain the programmes. At the end, SANP felt quite discouraged because although it had spent considerable time to establish linkages, nothing ultimately happened.

Despite these problems, the organisation has mobilised some resources from the government. In mobilising the government resources, the organisation places considerable importance to state government programmes. This is because there is less corruption in accessing resources from the state government as compared to that from the central government. Because of this reason, the instances of accessing state government programmes are many as compared to central government programmes (Table 7.3). The organisation has undertaken the activity of construction of roads in collaboration with the state government as part of Janmabhoomi Programme. Under this, a road was constructed in 1997 in Bompalli village with a total budget of Rs. 3 lakhs in which the SHG members had been associated. It also organised health awareness campaigns by showing video films. The District Medical Health Officer (DMHO) also allocated Rs. 70,000 for this programme.

Another major programme that the people themselves have taken up is DWCRA programme. During 1996 and 1997, a total of 375 households from 15 SHGs benefited from this programme (Table 7.3).

The NGO has linkages with government at various levels, as shown below.

- At the Mandal level, the organisation facilitated linkages with PHC, and DRDA.
- At the District level, SANP facilitated linkages with DRDA, SC, ST Corporation, DMHO, and district collector.

- At the State level, the linkages are with the Commissioner of rural development, DWCRA director, etc.
- At the Central level, the linkages are mainly with the National Environmental Board and Social Welfare Board.

Table 7.3: Resources mobilised by SANP since 1996

Year	*Activity*	*Source of funding*	*Number of villages covered*	*House-holds*
1996	• National Environment Board (Delhi)	Central	20	75
	• DWCRA/DRDA (Revolving Fund)	State	10	247
1997	• National Environment Board (Delhi)	Central	20	100
	• DWCRA/DRDA (Revolving Fund)	State	5	128
	• C.C. Road - Janmabhoomi, Health Awareness by Visual, Audio & Video (DMHO)	State	1	—
1998	• National Environment Board (Delhi)	Central	20	150

The contributing factors for the above linkages are as follows: (i) successful formation of village level women groups; (ii) strengthened savings and credit groups, as better participation of women in these groups have been observed; and (iii) regular participation of SANP staff in government meetings and rapport with committed government officials.

To some extent, the participation of the target group in PRIs also contributed to the process. Initially, the target group was not eager to participate in PRIs because they could not adequately recognise the importance of their participation and capturing of power at the local level. Due to capacity building inputs provided by the SANP the target group members have realised the benefits of their participation in PRIs to the community. A few members of groups promoted by the SANP became mandal panchayat members and village surpanches.

Strategies adopted

The organisation has adopted various strategies in establishing linkages with the government agencies both at central and state levels. The following may be highlighted as important ones:

- Meetings and regular interaction with concerned officials.
- Building up rapport through correspondence.
- Inviting the officials concerned for their meetings and training programmes to make them aware of the programmes implemented.
- Submission of appeals.
- Submission of projects and frequent reminders.
- Giving feedback on their present activities, the impact of the work, problems faced, etc.
- Forming NGO networks.
- Encouraging the people to involve themselves in local self-government at various levels.

The organisation enabled the people to become panchayat members, mandal panchayat members, education committee members, etc. In 21 villages, 300 persons contested for the above posts and 60 were elected to various positions in the 1995 election. By having the target group members in the PRIs, the organisation is of the opinion that many benefits and developmental programmes can easily be accessed by the people.

Of late, networking of NGOs at different levels is becoming an important strategy for many NGOs to establish critical linkages and influence the policies of the government in favour of the poor. The organisation is part of the district level network. It is not part of networks at the state, central and international levels. At the district level, the network is Dalit Voluntary Forum. Besides this, the organisation is part of the regional network of small initiative group network. The network was formed with 8 small NGOs, which shared the perspective and common concerns. These concerns include promotion of strategies for economic development, protection of tribal rights, environmental protection and re-generation, and strengthening PRIs in favour of the people. Under this network, meetings are conducted to discuss the problems, issues concerned and preparation of proper action plans. One of the objectives of this network is to develop interface with the government and mobilise local resources. Lobbying and advocacy with government and other major institutions at regional and state levels for proper policy is aimed.

Impact of interface on the target group

The organisation provides awareness to the target group members in the meetings conducted at the village level on various government programmes available and the procedures in obtaining these programmes. As noted earlier, SANP has also adopted certain strategies in accessing resources from the government. In this context, it is important to analyse the impact of its capacity building measures on the target group. In order to do that, we have collected information from 20 members of the self-help groups and male groups in Khammam, Nacherla, Pothureddypalli, Sivareddypalli and Jahingershabthanda. Of the 20 members, a majority belong to SCs and BCs. Most of these members are small and medium farmers (Table 7.4).

Table 7.4 : Socio-economic background of the sample households

Caste group/ Size-class	*Size of landholdings (%)*				
	Landless	*Marginal*	*Small*	*Medium*	*Total*
Backward Caste	—	—	66.67	33.33	30.00
Scheduled Caste	—	20.00	40.00	40.00	50.00
Scheduled Tribe	33.33	—	66.67	—	15.00
Others	—	—	100.00	—	5.00
Total	5.00	10.00	55.00	30.00	100.00
Actuals	1	2	11	6	20

The target group members obtained information on various government schemes such as housing, public distribution, bore well, crop loans, loans to live stocks, land distribution programmes from the organisation as well as other sources such as informal heads/village leaders government officials and public meetings. A majority of the sample members came to know of these programmes from government officials and informal village heads. Thirty per cent of the sample members reported that they came to know of the programmes from NGO or from leaders of self-help groups (Table 7.5).

Table 7.5 : Source of information on government programmes to sample respondents

Source of Information	*Total number of respondents*	*Percentage*
NGO	6	30
Govt. Officials	5	25
Informal heads/others	6	30
Public meeting	3	15
Total	20	100

A majority of the target group members are aware of the government programmes such as public distribution system, SC/ST corporation schemes, loans for agriculture, loans to rural artisans and TRYSEM, loans to acquire livestock assets (Table 7.6).

Table 7.6 : Knowledge of programmes and their utilisation

Particulars	*Percentage of members*		
	Aware of the programmes	*Availing the programmes*	*Utilising the programmes*
SC/ST Corporation Scheme	60	40	25
Borewell	60	50	30
Land distribution	35	30	10
Loans to acquire livestock	45	10	5
DWCRA	25	20	20
PDS	90	90	90
Loans to rural artisans and TRYSEM	50	25	30
Loans for agriculture	25	25	25
Others	65	40	40

Note : Others — Include children education loan, family planning loan, OAP, sanitary facilities, free education/free hostel.

Those who are aware of all the government programmes, have not obtained and utilised them effectively. This implies that the institutional capacity of many sample members has not yet built up in such a way that all of those who are aware of the programmes are able to obtain and utilise them. Moreover, those who availed the programmes, only few of them had productively utilised in the case of the public distribution system, loans for agriculture, rural artisans and TRYSEM.

From the discussion held with the sample respondents, it is reported that many of them had difficulties in establishing linkages and convincing the government officials concerned. Nonavailability of concerned government officials, lackadaisical attitude of the officials, bribing and inordinate delay to get work done, etc., were the problems faced by them. Among them, bribing and inordinate delay were the main difficulties faced by many respondents. For instance. Mr. Maisaiah and his wife in the project area reported that while obtaining loan of Rs. 75,000 for bore well from SC/ST Corporation they made not only several visits in a year but also bribed the concerned government officials with Rs. 3,000 to get the work done.

About 30 per cent of the sample members stated that they could independently approach the government officials for mobilisation of resources. Fifteen per cent of the sample members stated that they were dependent on the NGOs only for the time-being and could approach the officers independently in the long run. On the contrary, more than half of Sample members stated that they might have to depend on the NGO or need some assistance or help in approaching the government officials (Table 7.7). Some of the respondents stated that in a group they could establish linkages and access the resources but the same became difficult for individuals. For instance, "I alone cannot go out and meet the government officials but with the SANP people I can" stated Mrs. Sushilamma,

Table 7.7 : Independency/dependency of the target group members in approaching government officials in future

Particulars	*Total No. of respondents*	*Percentage*
Dependent on the NGO	4	20
Independent in approach	6	30
Dependent only for the time-being and can function independently in the long run	3	15
Need some assistance or escort	7	35
Total	20	100

At present, 70 per cent of the respondents still have to depend on the organisation for establishing linkages and access the resources from the government. This implies that there is still ample room for building institutional capacity of the target group members to establish improved interface in the days to come.

CONCLUSION

It can be noted that after the SANP's entry, the utilisation of the DWCRA revolving funds by the poor became effective, and the promotional activities relating to SHG stepped up. Prior to NGO entry, there was a lot of caste discrimination and not much group activity. But with the NGO involvement, caste discrimination came down, and groups became cohesive and strong. Of those who received benefits from the government, only a small proportion experienced positive impact. The percentage of the total resources mobilised from the government was not only very meagre but also declining. The proportion of the members depending on the NGOs for interface process was also large. These are the areas that the organisation wants to concentrate in the future.

NOTE

1. Although the organisation got registered in 1987 the development activities started only from 1994. Between 1987 and 1994, SANP focused on rapport building and social development as entry points. It was felt that such a rapport building would eventually benefit women and men in their integrated development. To be specific, the NGO concentrated on the following : (i) selection of villages on the basis of a socio-economic survey; (ii) conducting awareness camps on environment, health and education; (iii) non-formal education and adult education (with local contributions) for illiterate women; and, (iv) literacy programmes for non-school going children and school drop-outs.

8

Interface between Government Agencies and 'ACTS'

G. DASARATH REDDY & P. PUSHPA RANI

INTRODUCTION

Action for Community Service Society (ACTS), a registered NGO, has been working with the agricultural labourers, small and marginal farmers and women belonging to SC, ST and BC communities of Village Kota Mandal of Chittoor district, Andhra Pradesh. ACTS commenced its development activities in 1986 in 10 villages in this mandal and presently, it is working in 80 villages of the same mandal.

ACTS conducted a survey and had an elaborate discussion with the target community before formulating the development interventions. It identified issues like illiteracy, absence of organisations among them, powerlessness, assetlessness, inadequate access to credit for productive and consumption needs, ill-health, malnutrition, unemployment, gender discrimination, untouchability, degradation of environment as those on which development work should concentrate in the future.

Based on the survey conducted, the organisation formulated vision, mission and objectives. The vision of ACTS is to empower the most marginalised women belonging to *dalit*, tribal and backward communities for equal opportunities, gaining control over their income and improving their quality of life. The mission of ACTS is to educate, organise and capacitise the communities to undertake and sustain the activities leading to women's empowerment in due course of time.

The main objectives of the organisation are: (i) organising the rural poor through education and conscientisation; (ii) introducing different economic measures for their self-reliance; and, (iii) working for eco-society. The specific objectives of the organisation are to: (i) create a just, peaceful and non-exploitative society; (ii) increase the per capita income of the target population; (iii) eradicate illiteracy through formal and non-formal education programmes; (iv) develop leadership qualities among youth and women; (v) promote alternative community based credit delivery system to raise the income level of the rural poor; (vi) develop appropriate strategies to increase gender sensitivity; and, (vii) to increase the role of communities in conservation and sustainable use of natural resources.

Important activities are: (i) community organisation and conducting training programmes for SHG members in 75 villages and hamlets; (ii) promoting literacy for 1,000 school dropout children; (iii) thrift and credit for 4,000 women; (iv) natural resource management through watershed development in 4,000 hectares of land; and (v) mobilisation of resources from government and other institutions. In order to undertake these developmental activities, the organisation has 14 full-time staff and 50 volunteers.

ACTS has been forming village level organisations called thrift groups in the target area. By 1998-99, they had formed 99 women thrift groups for 3,750 women members in 80 villages. The coverage of the organisation in terms of number of villages, groups and members changed in the last few years. The number of villages covered by the organisation increased from 28 in 1994-95 to 80 in 1998-99; the growth has been particularly rapid from 1996-97. The total number of thrift groups increased from 35 in 1994-95 to 99 in 1998-99. Similarly, there has been rapid growth in the number of members. There has been, however, a change in the composition of groups and membership. While the organisation was working with both male and female thrift groups until 1996-97, it started to focus only on women groups from 1997-98 (Table 8.1). Thus, there has been a rapid growth in the number of groups and members in these groups; and the focus shifted to female groups in recent years. This growth was necessary to have a critical number of target group members which would become significant in the process of development and for making the programme sustainable. But, this has also posed a challenge as for as funding is concerned.

Table 8.1 : Progress of thrift groups in the project area of ACTS

Year	*No. of villages*	*Number of target groups*			*No. of target members*		
		Male	*Female*	*Total*	*Male*	*Female*	*Total*
1994-95	28	15	20	35	527	423	950
1995-96	28	18	35	53	687	892	1,579
1996-97	73	10	83	93	429	3,457	3,886
1997-98	75	—	93	93	—	3,500	3,500
1998-99	80	—	99	99	—	3,750	3,750

For undertaking the developmental activities, the NGO had depended on funds from both the government and external donors, and people's resources, namely, savings. Between 1995-96 and 1997-98, the organisation spent Rs. 74.78 1akhs on various developmental activities (Table 8.2). Of this amount, a bulk was mobilised from the state and central government agencies. Only 27.84 per cent of the total amount came from external donors. The information on changes in the distribution of funding across the sources in the last three years suggests that nearly half of the total funding came from external donors in 1995-96; the corresponding proportion was only less than 20 per cent in 1997-98. Thus, the organisation has come to rely heavily on resources from the state and central governments in recent years.

What are the contributing factors for this change in the dependence of the NGO on external funding? Since its inception, the organisation received funding from donor agencies such as Gandhi Peace Centre (EZE), CEBEMO (Netherlands), Oxfam and Inter-cooperation (Switzerland). The NGO benefited from these donor agencies as far as strengthening the capacity of the organisation and the target group was concerned. Oxfam helped them in the formation and consolidation of thrift groups. Similarly, it received considerable help from Inter-Cooperation in strengthening the thrift groups, sustainable agriculture and livestock development and management. The NGO was also not very much affected by the changing policies of donors; in fact, the policy changes suggested by the donors were helpful to the organisation and the target group.

Table 8.2 : Sources of funding for the organisation

(in Rupees)

Year	*State*	*Central*	*Donor*	*Total*
1995-96	347,600 (29.17)	267,325 (22.43)	576,720 (48.40)	1,191,645 (100)
1996-97	520,000 (22.12)	1,083,187 (46.07)	748,000 (31.81)	2,451,187 (100)
1997 -98	2,220,000 (57.88)	858,296 (22.38)	756,936 (19.74)	3,835,232 (100)
Total for three years	3,087,600 (42.62)	2,208,808 (29.54)	2,081,656 (27.84)	7,478,064 (100)

Note: Figures in parentheses are column-wise percentages.

While the NGO did not have problems with donor agencies *per se,* it encountered difficulty with one of the donors when a new person came to the helm of the agency. The organisation had difficulties with his style of functioning and his views on NGOs as a whole. In the opinion of the NGO, the present head of this donor agency had prejudice not only against the organisation but also the entire NGO movement. It became very difficult to work with the donors; and, hence, the organisation had to discontinue its partnership.

In the last 13 years or so, the NGO has realised that continuous dependence on external donors is not healthy. When funding from one donor comes to an end, one has to struggle to obtain resources for development from the same or different agency. In the experience of the NGO, one has to have 'godfathers' to get things done with donor agencies. Secondly, and more importantly, the policies of some of the donors abruptly change. Consequently, changes may have to be initiated in the programme in a short span of the period. This becomes very difficult.

Owing to these factors the organisation is putting efforts to make the programme self-sustainable. Now the plan of the organisation is such that all the programmes and activities evolved for the self-reliance and development of the target community become sustainable in the coming five years. The main source for the sustenance is thrift and credit programmes. At an estimated credit requirement of Rs. 7,500 per member per year, the total fund that needs to be generated is Rs. 3 crores. As of now, the people have contributed over Rs. 36 lakhs by way of savings, and the total credit fund is Rs. 87 lakhs (Table 8.3). It is estimated that the total amount of savings from the people will be rupees one crore in the next five years. An amount of Rs. 1.5 crores will be made available with the community. The gap of Rs. 50 lakhs is to be mobilised in the next five years to meet the credit needs of the women community members. The resources required to make the programme sustainable are expected to be mobilised from the government.

Table 8.3 : Resources (savings) mobilised from the members in thrift groups

Year	*No. of villages covered*	*No. of households benefited*	*Total thrift collected Rs.*	*Total funds available Rs.*
1995-96	75	1,300	749,272	1,700,000
1996-97	75	1,500	1,405,972	3,300,000
1997-98	75	1,800	2,500,000	5,700,000
Up to September 1998	80	1,000	3,640,000	8,700,000

The organisation is also exploring various ways in which the target group can mobilise the resources from the community to operate the government institutions provided for the community. In one of the villages, the youth mobilised resources to enable the government school to run effectively. The youth in a village have mobilised funds from the village *sanghas* by organising a benefit show. From this benefit show they got a profit of Rs. 10,000. The *sangha* members through ACTS have donated this amount towards the maintenance of Zilla Parishad school in the mandal. With these funds, the people are able to manage the school in their village.

The NGO is also making efforts to achieve institutional sustainability. As part of this, the target group is provided with training programmes in leadership and management skills, and in strengthening sustainable agriculture and allied agricultural activities. The organisation has also introduced nutrition for pre-school children and mother and child care programmes. The organisation is making efforts to mobilise the administrative expenses required to make the programme self-reliant on its own.

It is in this context that the need to generate resources from the government arises. To recapitulate the main points, in the context of donor uncertainty and changes in their policies, the NGO desires to make the people's programme sustainable. In this, a significant role is foreseen for resource mobilisation from the government. Hence, there is greater reliance on the resources obtained from state and central governments in recent years.

Interface with government agencies

According to ACTS, the government allocates resources under various programmes and schemes for the poor and down-trodden. But these resources are not efficiently used. The interface thus helps enabling the poor to access the resources available with the government and using the same efficiently for poverty alleviation.

ACTs feels that there is a strong need for interface between the government agencies and target groups of NGOs. People have every right to access the resources. NGOs which work for the poor can succeed to realise only 10 per cent of their objectives that they have set for themselves if they depend exclusively on resources obtained from donors. The remaining objectives can be met only through successful moblisation and utilisation of resources available with the government. While the NGOs are weak in terms of resources and manpower, the government has vast resources at its disposal. But, the government alone cannot handle all the programmes. In certain instances, government programmes failed to reach the poor; instead they created problems to the people. This is all because of the inability of the bureaucracy to develop rapport with the people. NGOs need to provide awareness and education on objectives and activities of the programmes, and enable the people to utilise the programmes successfully. Thus, interface is needed to minimise the deficiencies of each of the actors involved in development, and maximise the advantages of the institutions of development.

Establishing Linkages

The organisation seeks to facilitate the linkages at three levels; direct linkage with local government institutions and organisations such as Mandal Development Office (MDO), Mandal Revenue Office (MRO), Banks, Agricultural Office, veterinary hospital and Dairy cooperative, etc. At the district level, it seeks to facilitate linkages with the Collector, Joint Collector, Project Directors of District Rural Development Agency (DRDA) and Drought-Prone Area Programme (DPAP), etc. At the state level, it seeks to establish linkages with the Commissioner, Rural Development Department. At the Central level, contacts are sought to be established with the Secretaries and heads of various departments which provide resources for rural development and poverty alleviation. At the second level, it seeks to have linkages with various government departments through networks of NGOs formed around specific area and issues. At the third level, the people are expected to have linkages with various government agencies on their own. The required inputs in this regard will be provided by the NGO (Box 8.1).

Box 8.1: Helping the basket weavers through government linkages

In one of the villages, the basket weavers have been facing problems with regard to the procurement of raw materials and capital. The youth in this village identified a few such weavers belonging to the depressed castes. They raised funds from the weavers, and approached the Bamboo Basket Makers Cooperative Society of Y.C. Bandapalli in the Mandal for obtaining raw material for basket making. It took nearly 2 years for the group to have a savings account in the bank, and to get identified by the cooperative society. Finally, 150 basket weavers were identified and provided with assistance of Rs. 3,000 per family; of this amount, Rs. 1,600 was subsidy and the rest had to be repaid. After having linkages with the cooperative society, the raw material for the craft activity could be purchased at a lower price.

The linkages have had good impact on the mobilisation of resources. As noted earlier, the organisation mobilised about three-fourths of total funding in 1997-98 from the state and central government agencies. While mobilising the resources from the government, the organisation places considerable emphasis on both central and state government agencies, and a variety of programmes that are relevant for the organisation and its objectives (Table 8.4). Table 8.4, suggests that there is congruence between objectives and activities, and programmes mobilised from government agencies. Increasing the availability of credit fund for the members in the thrift groups, and enabling them to undertake income generating activities to increase incomes is one of the objectives. Hence, revolving credit fund was obtained from Rashtriya Mahila Kosh (RMK) in 1996-97 and 1997-98. Similarly, to fulfil the objective of conservation of natural

Table 8.4 : Programmes mobilised for the poor in the project area of ACTS

Year	*Programmes*	*Source of funding*	*No. of Villages covered*	*No. of households benefited*	*Total assistance (in Rs.)*
1995-96	DWCRA (Sheep)	State	6	90	90,000
	Petty traders	State	13	195	195,000
	DPAP	State	1	—	5,000
	Nutrition	State	14	14	12,600
	Non-formal education, MHRD, New Delhi	Central	50	1,000 (C)	267,325
1996-97	DPAP watersheds admn.	State	1 (P)	—	20,000
	DPAP Watersheds	-do-	14	42	400,000
	Basket Making/SVG	-do-	1	20	102,000
	DWCRA (petty traders)	-do-	1	—	42,000
	Dept. of Horticulture	-do-	1 (Con)	—	7,000
	Petty traders	-do-	3	42	42,000
	Horticulture	-do-	1	3	7,000
	CAPART, Housing Programme, New Delhi	Central	1	28	365,872
	Rashtriya Mahila Kosh, MHRD, New Delhi (Loan)	-do-	75	450	45,000
	Non-formal education	-do-	50	—	267,315
1997-98	DPAP watersheds	State	14	—	2,220,000
	Non-formal education, MHRD, New Delhi	Central	50	1,000(C)	408,296
	Rashtriya Mahila Kosh	-do-	75	371	450,000
1998-99	DPAP watershed works	State	10 (P)	5000 (ha)	3,600,000
	Administration of Watershed	State	100		330,000

Notes : C: Number of children;
P: Number of panchayats;
Con : Number of constituencies;
ha : Number of hectares.

resources and sustaining agriculture, the organisation got sanctioned watershed programmes from the state government in 1996-97, 1997-98 and 1998-99. To fulfil the objective of providing literacy to school drop-out children, resources were mobilised from the Ministry of Human Resource Development, New Delhi, in 1995-96, 1996-97 and 1997-98. The people also, on their own, mobilised resources from DWCRA programme. Thus, keeping the objectives and activities in view, resources have been mobilised from programmes of central and state governments.

Strategies Adopted

The NGO has adopted several strategies to mobilise the resources from the government :

- To make certain programmes like Janmabhoomi, literacy, Pulse Polio, etc., more successful, the NGO has helped the relevant government officials in the mobilisation of the people, and extending support to them.
- Whenever the government faced difficulty in solving some of the problems at the micro level, the NGO has extended its support in resolving them.
- The NGO provides awareness to the people on the programmes relevant to them. It builds the capacity of the people in approaching the officials concerned and in obtaining the resources.
- If the relevant officials do not recognise the efforts of an individual and/or a group in mobilising the resources, the NGO enables the people to undertake letter and signature campaigns. If these fail, they undertake *dharna* at the mandal, district and state levels. This strategy is adopted to put pressure on the government officials.
- The NGO does not approach the government for each and every programme. Before a decision is taken to approach the government, a careful study on the feasibility of a programme is done. This is because the government programmes tend to be time-target oriented, and at times, may be difficult to implement such programmes in short duration given the resources and capacity of the NGO. Hence, complete information about a programme is obtained before

a decision is taken to approach the government for the implementation of a programme.

- The NGO should have the willingness to go through difficult periods during the interface. The rules and regulations, and bureaucratic delays can cause widespread disappointment among the target group. The NGO needs to have an in-built strategy towards such situations. In a couple of issues relating to land, they had threats from vested interests and police. In one case, people were arrested and lathi charged. The NGO should have the willingness to face such problems.
- A continuous interface depends on certain good attributes of the NGOs and the way a sanctioned government programme was implemented. The field level performance needs to be convincing for the officials concerned. There needs to be accountability as far as the funds received from the government in terms of maintenance of accounts.

Box 8.2: The details of networks in which ACTS participates

Kuppam Constituency Network : At the mandal level, NGOs have formed this network. All the member NGOs meet whenever there is a problem in the constituency for discussion and resolution.

Swachanda Sansthala Samiakya (SSS) is a district level network. Normally, the meeting is held once a year; but, if there is any problem, the network does meet.

Consortium of NGO Network : Fifteen NGOs constitute this network. With meetings once in every two months, this network takes up common activities at the district level like environment, literacy, anti-arrack movement, etc.

Thrift Federation Network : All NGOs dealing with the thrift groups have formed themselves into a federation. . This network meets once in every three months to discuss the problems faced by thrift groups, government procedures, etc., and to take appropriate measures.

District Level Watershed NGO Association : This association meets once in every two months to discuss the OPAP policies and to check mis-utilisation of funds by the NGOs.

Rayalaseema Watershed Association (State Level) : This association meets once a year at different places to discuss issues relating to soil and water conservation.

State Thrift Cooperative Federation meets once a year to discuss about thrift groups and government policies.

- One of the important strategies adopted by ACTS is to participate and play an active role in the NGO network (Box 8.2). These networks were of considerable help in establishing and sustaining linkages with government agencies. Through the district level network of NGOs, the NGO could obtain resources for non-formal education. Similarly, the NGO networks helped obtain resources from DWCRA and watershed programmes.

Problems encountered in the interface

- To tap the central government resources, there should be somebody on behalf of the NGO to do some lobbying with the officials. Bribing officials (in percentage terms) at every stage is a major problem. Further, the organisation faces problems with regard to bureaucracy at every stage. Because of these problems, it is very difficult for the NGO to access central government funds.
- Often, grants from the government are not released on time.
- There are many rules and regulations to get a government programme sanctioned. The compliance of these rules and regulations is very difficult for a process-oriented NGO.
- Local political intervention and pressures are some of the other problems faced in the programme implementation.
- Local contractors of Village Kota Mandal unleash misleading propaganda about any programme that the organisation intends to implement, as they are the principal contenders to get such programmes sanctioned for execution.

Impact of interface on the target group

The organisation has had some success in the mobilisation of resources from the government agencies. But, there is great concern relating to building the capacity of the people. The organisation does provide awareness to the target group members on resources available in the government and how to access them. In order to see the impact of these capacity building measures, a questionnaire was canvassed among 20 members of thrift and credit groups in three villages. The questionnaire sought to obtain information on how they acquired information about government programmes and the impact of these programmes on income and employment of the households. Table 8.5 shows that a majority of these members belong to BCs and SCs, and are marginal, small and middle farmers.

Table 8.5 : The socio-economic background of the sample members of thrift groups

Caste groups/ size class	*Size of landholdings (%)*				
	Landless	*Marginal*	*Small*	*Medium & large*	*Total*
Scheduled Castes	—	15	—	10	25
Scheduled Tribes	5	—	10	—	15
Backward Castes	—	10	20	25	55
Other Castes	—	—	5	—	5
Total	5	25	35	35	100
Actuals	1	5	7	7	20

The sample members are aware of housing programmes from SC/ST corporation, borewells, loans for agriculture, livestock, DWCRA, etc. They came to know about these programmes in SHG meetings and from NGO staff. Government staff also played an important role in providing information (Table 8.6). Another interesting aspect is that there is a gap between the proportion of members who are aware of the programme and those who have actually availed in the case of DWCRA loans to rural artisans and agricultural loans. This reveals that those who are aware of the programmes have not been able to establish linkages and access the resources on their own. This has been due to several factors. In one of the cases, loan for borewell sinking could not be obtained as the land was registered in father's name, and transfer of legal right was expensive. In another case, the margin money was too high. But, in the case of majority, there was lack of follow up. This is some thing to which the organisation has to accord due attention to build the capacity of those who are unable to access the resources on their own. Nevertheless, those who have availed loan stated that they productively utilised the programme.

A majority of the sample members stated that the programme helped them in increasing employment and income. Of the 20 sample members, 16 reported that they could have increased employment and income on account of benefits received from the government. Three members, who had mobilised housing programmes, are now staying in government funded houses. Seven of 20 took loans to sink borewells. The borewell failed in one of the cases. In the case of others, there is substantial rise in income. Some stated that they could buy additional land, while one household invested the surplus on house construction. Six of the members took loans to purchase livestock. While in some of the cases this seemed to have resulted in increased income and employment. However, two of the members could not obtain any resource from the government.

Another noteworthy feature has been that the target group is now, by and large, independent in approaching the government officials for resources. Of the 20 sample members, nine stated that they could approach the government agencies on their own, while seven members stated that they were dependent on the NGO for the time being and could be independent in the future. Only four members stated that they were dependent on the NGO for establishing linkages with the government.

Table 8.6 : Knowledge and utilisation of government programmes

Name of the programmes	*Source of information*					*Percentage of members*	
	NGO	*SHG*	*Govt.*	*Village leaders & others*	*Total actuals*	*Availed*	*Productivity utilised*
SC/ST Corporation housing scheme	5	—	20	15	40	60	60
Borewell	5	—	20	—	25	40	40
DWCRA	25	15	—	—	40	30	30
Livestock	15	5	—	20	40	40	40
Loans to rural artisans	15	5	20	—	40	15	15
Sanitary facilities	—	—	—	—	—	10	10
Agricultural loans	5	—	25	20	50	40	40

CONCLUSIONS

This chapter brings out that uncertainties relating to external donor funds lead to restructuring of the programmes in favour of self-reliance and self-sustainability of people's organisations and development programmes initiated for the poor. An important role for local resource mobilisation is foreseen in such a strategic shift. Accordingly, the organisation has made several efforts to mobilise resources on its own and through the people. This chapter brings out that several strategies need to be adopted by the people and NGOs in local resource mobilisation. Particular emphasis is placed on developing certain attributes of NGOs such as accountability, convincing performance at the field level, etc. The primary data collected from a small sample of members in thrift groups shows that the capacity building initiatives had a positive impact on mobilisation and successful utilisation of government resources.

9

Interface between MARI (NGO) and Forest Department (APFD) in implementing JFM in Warangal North Division

MOHD. NOORUDDIN

INTRODUCTION

MARI is a Non-Governmental organisation working for the selected target communities in Warangal district of Andhra Pradesh since 1988. The organisation has been promoted by social workers who are committed to improve the condition of the poor. With the objective of integrated development of the selected target communities, the organisation has initiated a wide range of development programmes in Parvathagiri mandal of Warangal district. As the organisation started to gain momentum in the development process, it expanded its activities to Govinda Rao Pet and Tadwai tribal mandals of Warangal district which are located in the north division and the forest area of Warangal circle. In these two tribal mandals, the organisation has been focussing on operationalisation of the new concept of Joint Forest Management (JFM). An attempt has been made in this chapter to document the experiences of the organisation working with state and district level government offices of Forest Department.

The objectives of the organisation are : (i) to form community based organisations; (ii) to provide awareness and training to the community; (iii) to promote sustainable agriculture and forest management; and (iv) economic improvement of the poor. The important activities of the organisation are as follows: starting Community Self-Help Schools for the rehabilitation of child labourers; environmental education through Eco-Clubs in schools *(Prakruti Chetana* Project); collaborating with the government for implementing District Primary Education Programme for the eradication of child labour; Implementation of JFM, promotion of Self-Help Groups for women belonging to weaker sections; skill and economic development activities; Krishi Vedikas (Farmers' Associations) to promote sustainable agriculture including non-chemical approaches to pest management; seed production to promote farmer's self-sufficiency in agriculture; vermiculture, tank renovation and other natural resource development activities to enhance the productive capacity of the poor people's resources; Farmer's Co-operative societies; promoting awareness and infrastructure related to drinking water, sanitation, health and hygiene; special activities for the empowerment of tribals, *dalits* and women; and bridging linkages between community and government and enhancing community capacity to mobilize government support for poverty alleviation.

In this connection, the organisation collaborated with the following departments in implementing the programmes (Table 9.1).

Joint Forest Management

Andhra Pradesh has about 6.37 million hectares of forest area which is expected to be brought under the model of JFM. The forests in Andhra Pradesh are in a seriously degraded condition. A significant proportion of the area officially designated as forests are degraded to varying degrees, some of the area being without any trees, shrubs or even grass. Estimates made by the Forest Department, which are based primarily on remote sensing data, show that about 25 per cent of the designated land is without any forest cover. Trends over time show continuing rampant destruction. As a result of this destruction, livelihood of the poor depending upon forest is facing a grave threat besides serious problems relating to agricultural production.

The organisation plans to collaborate with the forest development with the objective of developing the livelihood opportunity of the poor and aims at addressing the following issues: (i) conservation

Table 9.1 : Linkages with government departments

Sl.No.	Department	Programme	Coverage
1.	Ministry of Environment, Government of India, New Delhi	National Environment Awareness Campaign	The entire project area
2.	-do-	Eco-clubs	40 schools
3.	Spices Board, Cochin	Promotion of cultivation of quality chillies and developing infrastructure.	NA
4.	DSE, Government of AP	District Primary Education Programme	NA
5.	District Administration Government of AP	Child Labour Rehabilitation Project	NA
6.	SC Corporation and District Administration Government of AP	Dairy programme	100 SC households
7.	DRDA and SC Corporation	Formation of DWCRA groups and SC women Government of AP	38 DWCRA groups self-help groups 15 SC SHGs
8.	NABARD	Support for women SHGs	6 women SHGs
9.	State Directorate of Youth Services	Youth Development Programmes	NA
10.	Andhra Pradesh Forest Department	JFM promotional work	NA
11.	Government of AP	Rural Sanitation Infrastructure Development Programme	NA
12.	MHRD, Government of India	Environmental Education Programmes in Schools	NA

Note: NA - Not Available

and development of forests with a view to protecting and widening the livelihood opportunities of the poor depending on forests; (ii) protecting the agricultural production resource base of the people living in and around forest areas; and, (iii) empowering the communities for sustainable management of the local forests, which is the prime natural resource.

While examining the feasibility and ambience for successfully operationalising the JFM concept, the following factors need to be kept in mind. The declared National Forest Policy (1988), the government order on JFM and special memo of the Chief Minister of the state provide the policy framework. The *'Diktats'* of the World Bank, which is providing fund to the tune of Rs. 360 crores to Andhra Pradesh Forestry Development Projects, also shape the policy framework. The experiences of successful participatory forest management experiences emerging from other states like West Bengal and new voices in the Forest Department of AP suggesting participatory forest management also provide a favourable environment. There is loss of true access and control of forest areas under the Andhra Pradesh Forest Department (APFD) forest areas due to extremist activities.

Despite the above conducive atmosphere, operationalisation of JFM concept in its true spirit is yet to get the required pace. Further, there are serious conceptual aberrations in the implementation. NGOs, without becoming tail to the government and without restricting to mere intermediary role should be able to function as impeccable and strong organisations representing people's will and ideas. NGOs, like MARI, should have the capacity to replace the official JFM with people's JFM (Box 9.1).

Specific objectives of MARI for taking up JFM promotional project

- To motivate and guide people to form people's Forest Protection Committees in at least about 20 villages (Table 9.2) and thus focus on about 10,000 hectares of forest land for protection and development of participatory approaches.
- To train and enhance the skills, capacities and leadership of people's protection committees, to function as harmonious and effective forest protection and management committees and to guide them to evolve proper benefit sharing mechanisms.

Table 9.2 : Details of SHGs of JFM promotional project during 1997

Year	*No. of villages*	*No. of SHGs*	*No. of SHG members*	*Total savings Rs.*	*Matching grants Rs.*
1997	10	9	255	171,840	101,000
1998	10	16	641	246,840	168,000

Box 9.1: Perspective of Joint Forest Management

Present Official Perspective of JFM	**Perspectives for people's JFM**
JFM in isolated pockets	Contiguous area approach
Confined to targets	Widespread people's movement
Fund for investment on labour works is central attraction	Returns and rights
Rigid scientific treatment practices—mockery of micro-planning	Lead role to people's knowledge and ideas and true participation of dependent communities
Capital intensive plantation treatment operations	Low cost natural regeneration and protection
Narrow partnership	Ownership orientation
Economic incentives to divert the dependency on forest	Poverty alleviation within the forest areas
Equal stakes	Stakes on equity principles
Market pressures on forest ignored	Strategies to encounter market pressures on forest
Exclusive forest management	Positive biotic interface

- To develop a healthy relationship, mutual trust, respect and confidence between people and forest department.
- To create successful and sustainable models of participatory forest management which can have a wider replicability.
- To promote the people's awareness on JFM and build a people's movement for forestry management and protection in Warangal district.
- To motivate the community to take necessary action to prevent illegal forest felling by timber smugglers and for saving the forests from forest fires.
- To organise effective women groups to ensure their fullest participation in JFM related activities and establish special rights for women belonging to landless and poor families.
- Sharing skills and expertise with other NGOs interested in taking up JFM promotional work.

Outreach of the organisation and JFM promotional interventions

The organisation has educated the people in Govinda Rao Pet and Thadvai mandal ranges of Warangal district about the concept of JFM. It has also motivated them to participate in JFM and formed *Vana Samrakshna Samithis* (VSSs). In this range, the JFM is covering 20 villages under 8 grama panchayats. About 2,025 families and 10,320 people are being covered under this project. Out of the total population, 70 per cent belong to ST (Koya) , 10 per cent to SC, and remaining to other categories. The total forest area being covered under this project is around 10,490 hectares. The major occupations of the people in the area are agricultural labour, and collection of Non Timber Forest Produce (NTFP).

The organisation is helping the 20 VSSs formed in this area in protecting the forest area from grazing, fires and smugglers. It is also helping and guiding the VSSs in various development operations like copying, singling, thinning, removing unwanted species, soil and moisture conservation. The NTFP like beedi leaves, tapsi, etc., has increased significantly due to protection of forest from fires and grazing.

Factors contributing to interface

- Promoting livelihood opportunities of the poor, through sustainable development and management of natural resources, is central to the vision of the organisation. Hence, the organisation was prepared to face any amount of hardship and accept any amount of responsibility to operationalize the concept of JFM in Warangal district. This determination and readiness of the organisation was realised and recognised by the Forest Department and they started appreciating its active involvement.
- Initially, the organisation accepted all the responsibilities given by the Forest Department. The staff of the organisation had even participated in the midnight raids conducted by special squads of Forest Department to check smuggling.
- Even before the JFM work began, the organisation had good interaction with social forestry and wildlife wings of the Forest Department and the work done by the organisation

had won the appreciation of the Department. This goodwill did help in developing proper relationship with the territorial staff connected with JFM work.

- Initially, when the staff of the Forest Department independently approached the local communities with the idea of implementing JFM by formation of VSS, the people were highly critical of the Forest Department and held the officials responsible for forest degradation. People were very skeptical about the Department and they did not show any enthusiasm. When MARl entered into the process, it conducted cultural programmes specially developed on JFM themes, and organised a series of meetings to enable the tribal communities understand the potential development opportunities that JFM can create for them. When MARl succeeded in drawing forth excellent response to JFM from local communities, the department started giving more importance to its involvement in the whole process of implementing JFM.
- The staff of the organisation has easy access to villages located in interior high forest areas while such an access is not there for the officials of Forest Department due to intensive operations of militant political groups. The organisation has made all the necessary effort in these villages and formed good VSSs. With this, the Forest Department has realised the special advantages of involving an NGO in the JFM process.
- The organisation staff have participated in a number of trainings, workshops, review meetings, exposures at the state and national levels and have gained a thorough understanding of the concept of JFM and participatory forest management and the diverse field experiences of the same. The participation at the state level review meetings exposed the NGO to the pertinent issues concerning the process of building people's movement on JFM. Thus, works and the thorough understanding of the concept and deep insights into the actual process helped the organisation to play an influencing role at the district level. The department staff respected and valued the NGO role.

- Foresters who have so far done a nasty policing job were neither mentally ready nor did they have skills to play the role of facilitators to build people's forestry management models. Thus, NGO involvement was felt necessary to bridge the gaps between staff of the department, particularly at the lower level and the programme.
- The organisation has always restrained from indiscriminate condemning, criticism, and negating of APFD staff, rather it has appreciated their technical knowledge and skills in forestry. Right from the guard level, the NGO was dealing individually by way of offering constructive criticism, feedback and suggestion to improve their functioning. On some serious matters or issues related to the performance of lower level staff, the organisation usually discussed with the District Forest Officer and Conservator who were dealing with their subordinate staff in their own way.
- Whenever there was a need to question the functioning, actions or lack of initiative of the whole department, the organisation was enabling the communities to raise such issues. This approach helped to minimise direct confrontation and avoid personalisation of issues. Thus, the organisation continued to work together despite differences and confrontation on issues.
- When the World Bank review missions and senior departmental officials from the state Forest Department visited north division of Warangal, they were appreciative of the progress of JFM. Local officials who were conscious of the support extended by the organisation in achieving such progress continued to give importance to the organisation's interface.
- Regular VSS meetings, proper maintenance of books and records, proper systems for transparency and accountability, preparation of people's microplans, trainings, cultural programmes for people's motivation, community organisation and regular monitoring, efforts to address gender and equality concerns resulted in creating strong VSSs. Having seen the quality of VSSs promoted by the organisation, the forest department has become very cooperative and has recognised MARI as an essential actor in the whole process.

- The policy framework of the government order on JFM, Andhra Pradesh Forestry Development projects, *Diktats* of the World Bank and positive attitude of higher officials towards NGOs were also some of the important factors that allowed NGOs like MARI to intervene into forestry management.
- Pressures on the local Forest Department officials to achieve targets also forced them to collaborate with NGOs which could help them in this process.
- Networking of VSSs at the range level, regular review meetings and interaction with the DFO and Conservator at the district level planning and coordination meetings at the division level have helped the organisation in sustaining and further strengthening the interface with forest department for the successful promotion of JFM. Particularly, the practice of evolving joint plans made the forest department committed and the department was obligated to address the planned activities. Thus, the forest department and the organisation were working together on the common agenda to the environment.

Problems faced

During the last few years, in the process of working with the forest department for the effective implementation of the concept of JFM, the organisation had faced problems relating to: capacities in fulfilling responsibilities of all the concerned actors; the process and strategy adopted for operationalisation of JFM concept; and the external forces influencing the JFM process (including the functioning of other line departments). To solve these problems, the following steps have been taken up:

- Effective (regular and clear) co-ordination and communication between all the concerned actors.
- Monthly meetings of VSS federation at the range level.
- Constant interaction with mass media and exposing the process to public at large.
- Regular discussions with Range Officer, DFO, and Conservator.

- Continuous dialogue with political parties including extremist groups.
- Dissemination of information to strengthen public vigilance of the process.
- Discussions in the District Forest Committee meetings.
- Discussion and highlighting the issues at the state level NGO network meetings and APFD review meetings by the Forest Department, AP.
- Organising VSSs to take issues to the notice of the state level senior officials and lobbying at the state level.
- Pressurising the forest department to commission enquiries and/or fact-finding process to check corruption and abuse of project implementation.
- Process documentation and records maintenance to ensure transparency and accountability.

CONCLUSION

Though there were some problems at the initial stage, the organisation has been able to improve proper interface with the forest department for effective operationalisation of the new concept of JFM. Recognition and acceptance of each other's strengths and weaknesses, mutual commitments, respect, trust, confidence, appreciation and constructive criticism are the basic aspects which strengthened the interface. The forest department, MARI and local community are happy about the progress of JFM in the area. The experiences generated prove that JFM can be a very successful model. The experiences also reveal that improved interface between the government and field based NGOs can surely multiply the pace and results of development interventions and such process can also be of great learning for NGOs and government.

10

Government and Target Group Members of Grama Vikas in Mulbagal Taluk of Kolar District

M.V.N. RAO & R.R. BIRADAR

INTRODUCTION

Grama Vikas is a NGO working in Mulbagal taluk of Kolar district since 1979. The organisation started working with "welfare approach" by launching a nutrition food programme aimed at integrated child development. With the passage of time, the needs felt by the people and issues in the area led Grama Vikas to shift its focus from welfare to development. The new approach basically intends to ensure sustainable and self-managed development process, and to empower the marginalised women by forming self-help groups. Since then, the organisation has devoted, and committed itself to accomplishing integrated sustainable rural development by initiating multi-disciplinary developmental activities in the region.

Grama Vikas states "unless we stop resources in rural areas going out—be it human, natural, economic, or cultural—no rural development is possible"[1]. The government, both Central and States, has also launched several development programmes since independence. Unfortunately, neither has made it possible for the weaker section of the society to enjoy the benefits provided by the government nor has the government shown keen interest to reach the benefits to the real the benefits to the real poor. Thus, the fruits of development activities have largely gone to the better-off, and the poor are becoming poorer as they are deprived of many state provided goods and services which are meant for improving their living location. This has provided space for NGOs to play a catalytic role in seeing that the benefits reach the real poor. Therefore, the NGO has to facilitate the interface with government and enable the target group to establish linkages with various line departments. Against this background, this chapter intends to analyse the factors contributing to the interface, the strategies adopted in accessing the resources, the problems faced by the organisation while dealing with various government departments. Above all, the perceptions of the target group members on interface process have also been analysed.

ABOUT THE ORGANISATION

The organisation came into existence in response to local problems such as chronic droughts, deteriorating environment, severe poverty and unemployment, deplorable life of women belonging to backward castes, substantial number of children suffering from lack of nutritious food[2], deteriorating condition of tanks, etc.

The goal of Grama Vikas is 'empowering marginalised rural women with special emphasis on children, environment and networking with rural women's associations to accomplish sustainable development through food security'. Therefore, children, women and environment are said to be the pillars of the organisation. Thus, the main objective of the organisation is integrated rural sustainable development which includes children, women, and natural resources as its important constituent part of development.

The specific objectives of the Grama Vikas are:

- to improve health and nutritional aspects so as to minimise child and antenatal mortality;
- to organise and build children's and women's organisations at the grass roots level;
- to promote income generation activities for women. The idea is that once economic empowerment is ensured the status of women in the family will improve;
- to empower women through awareness programme and self-employment;

- to fight for women's rights and against social evils and injustice;
- to promote SHGs, and thereby encourage savings and credits activities among poor women;
- networking with other NGOs in the district to chalk out an action plan for women's empowerment and rural development; and,
- protection and sustainable management of natural resources.

Area of operation and staff members

Grama Vikas has been working in Kolar district covering 112 villages, of which 100 are in Mulbagal taluk, and the rest in Bangarpet taluk. These villages are divided into 15 clusters. The main project office is located at Honnesettihalli which is 15 kms. away from the taluk headquarters.

The organisation has a total staff of 50 members. Among them 15 are institutional development facilitators, 19 self-help facilitators, 11 administrators, 3 internal auditors and the rest are training and sector coordinators. Each of the clusters has one cluster organiser and one or two community organisers (depending on the size of the cluster) to carry out various development activities.

Target group

SHGs are formed for women belonging to socially and economically backward sections. Most of them are poor and marginalised who are involved in one or the other economic activities. Moreover, by promoting Parent's Federation (PF), men are also encouraged to take up some community activities and play a supportive role to the SHGs formed by women. The number of SHGs increased from 114 in 1996 to 172 in 1998 (Table 10.1).

Table 10.1: Operational details of the Grama Vikas

Year	*Number of villages covered*	*Number of clusters*	*Number of SHGs (female groups)*	*Target group members (female)*
1996	104	15	114	3,488
1997	104	15	116	3,592
1998	112	15	172	3,790

MAIN ACTIVITIES OF THE ORGANISATION

The following are the important activities initiated by the organisation in the project area.

Integrated child development

Grama Vikas believes that "the children are the asset for the nation and without whose integrated development the women's empowerment would not take place", in the sense that if a child falls sick then the mother will not be able to take part in the socio-economic activities. Under this programme, various children-related activities have been taken up. Some of the important activities are providing nutritious food, supplementary education, and health care activities.

Women's empowerment and development

Women have been neglected in most respects especially in the decision-making process and participation in rural development. Grama Vikas believes that "no rural development is possible unless women are given freedom to play an active role in the socio-economic activities". If women are not given freedom to participate in economic activity, no empowerment can be achieved and she will be overlooked from any decision to be taken by men. In a bid to achieve the women's empowerment and to make them participate in income generating activities, the organisation has introduced both income and employment intensive activities.[3]

Natural resource development and management (NRDM)

The organisation believes that "unless soil, water and vegetation are protected, the future of rural India is very bleak and dismal". In this context, Grama Vikas has undertaken important activities like soil and water conservation, desilting of tanks, silt application on dry lands so as to promote organic farming to increase the crop yields and so on. Through these activities, Grama Vikas hopes to achieve sustainable development of agriculture and food security.

Source of funding

The organisation was initially supported by OXFAM, UK based donor agency, for many of its activities. While there was a gradual shift in its approach from welfare to development, the organisation came into contact with some other donor agencies such as NOVIB, Christian Children's Fund (CCF), Community Aid Abroad and Swiss Development Cooperation-Inter Cooperation (SDC-IC). A larger proportion of fund was mobilised from the government. (Table 10.2).

Table 10.2: Sources of funds mobilised from different agencies in 1997-98

Name of the agency	*Total amount (Rs.)*	*Percentage*
NOVIB (Holland)	3,674,497	14.59
Christian Children's Fund (U.S.A)	3,917,667	15.55
SDC-IC (Switzerland)	477,350	1.89
Self (GV)	4,467,590*	17.73
Government	12,656,440	50.23
Total	25,193,544	100.00

Note : * The information on funds existing with Grama Vikas pertains up to March 1999.

INTERFACE WITH GOVERNMENT DEPARTMENTS

The passive role of the government in the fair delivery system of goods and services to the poorest section of the rural society largely influenced the organisation to join hands with various line departments in the region. The organisation which was mainly involved in mobilising the disadvantaged group of rural women in the region has been successful in establishing rapport and good contact with the government departments after its 3-4 years of functioning.

The organisation states that the government as a part of rural development programmes provides many benefits for the people. However, most of the poor are deprived of the benefits of the government programmes and opportunities. They are also unable to participate in the decision-making bodies, and are becoming worst victims of market fluctuations, unemployment and poverty. These factors paved the way for Grama Vikas to interfere and interface with the government departments to build linkages to ensure the smooth functioning of government delivery system at various levels and mobilise the resources channelising toward the benefits of the poor.

As per the understanding of the organisation, the concept of linkages is as follows: linkage process involves bringing the poor and the government together and making the officials understand the problems of the poor, and respecting them. It also involves enabling the poor to easily access the resources from the government and ensure the sustainability of the programmes. The organisation believes that building and maintaining the contact with the government officials has great in-built potential to make the poor approach and access the resources from the government.

ACCESSING THE GOVERNMENT PROGRAMMES

The organisation has built up linkages with various line departments to enable the rural poor to approach and access the resources from both local and central governments. As a result of which the departments have started understanding the aims, objectives and the activities of the organisation which seem to be similar. It is with the growing popularity and pioneering works concerned with women in the rural areas that the government departments have been impressed and have come forward to implement a few programmes from the central and local governments with the support of the organisation (Table 10.3).

Contributing factors

The linkages are mainly collaborating, extending infra-structural facilities and building the capacity of members of SHGs. The following are some of the important contributing factors to establish linkages with the government departments.

- Most of the government officials are not aware of the on-going and newly launched anti-poverty programmes. With a view to publicising and making them aware of the programmes, and the needs of the poor, the organisation has started building the linkages by providing knowledge and information.
- With a view to ensuring the sustainability of the people-oriented development process, improved linkages are needed to be established with various line departments especially local organisations concerning the needs of the rural poor, so that the government programmes can be made sustainable in yielding the results.

Table 10.3: Government programmes accessed during 1996 to 1998

Year	*Name of the programme*	*State/ Central*	*No. of villages covered*	*No. of households benefited*	*Total assistance (in Rs.)*
1995-96	IRDP scheme		12	29	240,000
	SC/ST Development Corporation (DWCRA)		15	19	160,000
	Housing scheme	State	2	20	50,000
	Anganawadi building		3	14	280,000
	Milk Cooperative Society		1	79	20,000
	Community Buildings		1	95	–
	SHGs linkage programme	(NABARD)	3	–	75,000
			42	630	1,634,500
1996-97	Primary school building		7	1	1,380,000
	Housing		15	92	–
	Mini-water supply		3	1	–
	Bhagya Jyothi lights		19	150	40,000
	Anganwadi		2	85	100,000
	DWCRA	State	4	40	45,000
	Sanitation		4	225	282,500
	Milk dairy		1	84	432,000
	Loans from SC/ST Development Corporation		23	48	242,000
	IRDP loan		30	45	2,072,200
	Bank linkage programme (NABARD)		45	550	
1997-98	DWCRA		7	70	175,000
	Loan from SC/ST Development Corporation		20	50	40,000
	IRDP		40	80	640,000
	Housing scheme	State	52	185	3,700,000
	Electric facility		20	85	–
	Mini water supply		6	500	–
	Community building		5	350	150,000
1998	Grain storage by Save Grain Campaign and Department of Food procurement and distribution	Central	41	291	79,514,40

- In future, the organisation may have to transform its role. For this to happen, the people's organisations and the government departments should come closer. The target members need to understand the resources available with the government, and the government should understand the needs of the poor, respect them and initiate programmes to fulfil them.
- In view of the recent changes in the democratic decentralised government, local level planning, implementation and monitoring of the programmes by the local people become important elements of development process. The organisation seeks to play a facilitated role to enable the poor to participate in the development process at various levels by working with the decentralised government.
- The decentralised government at the village level has been provided with plenty of resources to initiate local level development programmes. To tap these resources and channelise towards the benefit of the poor, the linkage becomes essential.
- In identifying the genuine beneficiaries for various government programmes, the organisation has started guiding the officials.
- If the people's involvement is more in the development process the policies can easily be changed in favour of the poor. This is true of women also. Therefore, this requires motivating the poor and women towards development.
- The organisation has already initiated various development programmes organising the rural women in the form of SHGs. Being aware of this, the government officials have come forward to provide a few programmes which, otherwise, the government itself would have launched and implemented.
- It is the experience of the government officials that the programmes which have been implemented, monitored and at times evaluated by the government departments have not yielded fruitful results. Therefore, if the programmes are implemented through the organisation, better impact on the socio-economic status of the poor can be achieved.

- Most of the villages, where the organisation is functioning, are far away from all-weather roads. Hence, the implementation, frequent monitoring and evaluation of the programmes become difficult for the concerned government officials. For this reason, they want collaboration to implement such programmes through the organisation.
- If the implementation and the follow-up are done by both the agencies, the degree of effectiveness of the programme often tends to be better. Therefore, both the actors agree to work together.
- The unique performance and popularity of the organisation towards the improvement of the rural poor in the region would have made the government officials to understand the aims and objectives of the organisation and come forward to launch some programme on experimental basis.
- Demonstration, conduct of procession by *Mahila Samavesh*, and publicising its organisational efforts to bring the disadvantaged group of rural women on one platform and seeking to improve their socio-economic status in the society have influenced the government officials to extend their support.

Strategies adopted

The organisation has shown keen interest in working with various government departments with a view to ensuring improved delivery system of the government in providing goods and services to the poor. In view of this, the organisation has adopted several strategies to establish good relationship and rapport with several line departments in the region. They are :

- conducting people's meetings and inviting the MLAs and the concerned government officials. These meetings have given an opportunity to the government officials to have direct dialogue with the rural people, especially targetted group of the poor women;
- providing basic facilities such as transport, pandals, convenient place to conduct meetings, food, etc., to government officials while conducting the meetings with the people;

- attending seminars/workshops organised by various government departments and presenting the progress of the organisation and its vision and mission towards rural development;
- keeping regular contact with the government officials, and having a friendly dialogue relating to generic issues whenever they come into contact with them; and
- sending letters to the government officials inviting them to participate in the functions, meetings, etc.

Problems encountered

Though the government officials have shown concern about the poor in extending their support, the organisation has faced problems while dealing with various line departments of the local and central governments. The routine problems faced by the target group members while accessing programmes from the government are: (*i*) stating that application forms are exhausted mainly to avoid the work load; (*ii*) very frequently, the officials state that the submitted applications are missing and cannot be traced; in such cases, new applications have to be submitted; (*iii*) cumbersome and time consuming procedures adopted in processing the applications and scrutinising the loan requests; (*iv*) demanding bribes at various stages of work; and (*v*) frequent visits and meeting the officers for follow-up, and making applicants to run from pillar to post. All these problems discourage the poor women establish linkage and access the resources from the government. This shows that the officials are not interested in giving them assistance.

The NGO is a member of KOVON, the network of NGO located at Kolar and FFVORD K, the network NGO at the state level. The network NGO discusses the common action plan such as anti-arrack movement, sustainable agriculture development, etc. However, as of now, the network NGOs are not moving towards any advocacy and lobbying as such. But in future, they are going to have a critical discussion on public policies so as to change them in favour of the rural poor.

PERCEPTION OF TARGET GROUP MEMBERS

In the process of obtaining the government resources, the organisation has enabled the poor women to approach and access the government programmes on their own. How far the target group members are able to learn the lessons and build up their institutional capacity? To address this question, data on perceptions on interface were collected from 20 women sample members. These women obtained different government programmes, and have randomly been selected from three villages covered by the organisation.

Most of the sample members were landless and marginal farmers belonging to the SC/ST communities. These sample members were the beneficiaries of NABARD linkage programme, SC/ST development corporation programme and tank desiltation programme which were the main programmes accessed from the government and implemented through the organisation. The information was collected on how many of the sample members were aware of the government programmes, how many of them applied, obtained and put into productive use. More than half of the sample members were aware of the basic facilities provided by the government such as housing, drinking water, bhagya jyothi, sanitary programmes, public distribution system (PDS) etc.; little less than half of the sample members were aware of the poverty alleviation programmes, such as IRDP, SC/ST Development Corporation programme, and tank desiltation, provision of subsidised seeds and fertilizers from the agricultural department. Moreover, one-fourth of the beneficiaries were aware of social security programmes such as Old Age Pension (OAP), loan towards handicapped, widower pension and very few of them were aware of the programmes relating to agricultural activities such as Ganga Kalyan Yojana, storage bins, plantations, etc.

The analysis brings out the fact that all of those who were aware of the programmes had not been able to obtain the programmes from the government. Some of the sample members accessed the programmes. Moreover, a very few of them who obtained the programmes were able to make use of it and derive better results. This follows that these sample members who were all aware of the programmes were not able to apply, access all the programmes and put into productive utilisation, indicating that the sustained interface was still lacking.

While approaching and accessing the resources from various departments the sample members encountered some problems caused by the officials. Half of the sample members did not encounter any problems as the group animator took care of the whole process. The problem of frequent visits and meeting the officials, inordinate deferment in sanctioning the loan amount, mobilisation of the necessary certificates from various places and offices, and afraid of having a dialogue with the officials and so on were faced by the members.

The discussion held with the respondents reveals that most of the sample members who had obtained loan for tank desiltation and applied to their farm field reported that there was an increase in the productivity per acre. A few of them who had obtained loan for animal husbandry said that there was a continuous and steady increase of income to support their family. Very few of the sample members had misutilised the programme. Out of the 20 sample members, a majority of them had repaid the loan amount.

The information on whether the poor could independently approach the government agencies has been provided in Table 10.4. It is noted that out of the 20 sample members of target groups, a majority of them were confident, independent in approaching the government officials and access the programmes/facilities meant for themselves in future, while one-fourth needed initial support of the organisation to establish linkages with the concerned line departments. However, 5 members were not confident in approaching and accessing the programme and 2 were entirely dependent on the organisation to establish linkages and access the programmes even in the days to come.

Table 10.4: Approaching the government officials

Particulars	*Total number of respondents*	*Percentage*
Confidence in approaching	5	25
Independence in approaching	8	40
Entirely dependent on Grama Vikas	2	10
Initial dependency on Grama Vikas	5	25
Total	20	100

CONCLUSION

It is clear from the foregoing discussion that with a view to ensuring sustainable and self-mannaged development process and empower the marginalised women, the organisation started several activities and programmes mobilising from both State and Central governments by involving the target group members. To build the institutional capacity of the people and enable them to establish linkages and sustained interface with the government officials, the organisation has provided information on various government programmes, the places where these can be accessed, procedure and the like. Many a time, the staff of the organisation have taken the lead and accompanied the target group members while accessing the resources from the government. It is obvious that those who were all aware of the programmes had not applied, accessed and put into productive utilisation. This implies that the capabilities of all the sample respondents had not yet been built up in such a way that they were able to approach the government departments on their own to get their things done. However, it is clear that a majority of those who had obtained the programmes stated that they benefited from the assistance. But, at present a little over one-third of the sample respondents are dependent on the NGO to establish linkages and access the available resources from the government. Building women's empowerment and establishing sustained interface with the government departments in the market driven economy is the main issue for the organisation.

NOTES

1. The ideological view of rural development was evolved by late Dr. N.K.A. Iyer, the founder member of the organisation. Late Dr. Iyer was from near the village Ganjigunte, Andhra Pradesh. He did his post-graduate and doctoral work in environment in Washington University. He was basically an environmentalist and looked carefully at rural life from a different point of view. He was greatly stirred by the rural poor children suffering from under-nutrition.
2. The Indian Population project has pointed out that a large number of children found in the district were suffering from malnutrition. See the report of the Indian Population Project, 1979.
3. Some of the activities worth mentioning are: savings and credit activities through the promotion of SHGs; income generation activities through community banking; linking SHGs with banks to take up individual/community based activities; social action programmes; awareness and skill-building programmes so as to strengthen their institutional capacity; dissemination of information of various government programmes; conducting training programmes and exposure visits; networking of women organisations at different levels; and discussing the issues related to women's empowerment and development.

11

Interface between Government and Target Group Members of NGOs

A Case Study of GRAMA

D.M. SRIDHAR & R.R. BIRADAR

INTRODUCTION

Gramina Abhivruddhi Mathu Adhyayana Kendra (GRAMA) is a NGO involved in the empowerment of rural women towards reduction of poverty and unemployment, and in integrated rural development. GRAMA believes that any reduction of rural poverty is mainly dependent on the socio-economic and political empowerment of rural women through formation and promotion of SHGs. Since its inception[1] in 1990, GRAMA has been focusing on empowerment of rural women by initiating micro finance and income generation activities, with a view to bringing about socio-economic equality among the rural poor. GRAMA organises the poor women into Credit Management Groups (CMGs), which act as a platform for fulfilling the vision and mission of the organisation.

The organisation visualises "a society where every individual irrespective of his/her socio-economic and gender identity, is assured of his/her basic rights, and discharge the corresponding responsibility operationalised within a sustainable environment". The mission of the organisation is "to dedicate itself to empower the self-sustainable people's institutions so as to enable all people to participate actively in the decision-making process on matters which affect their lives".

Keeping this vision and mission, the organisation has chosen Chitradurga district as an arena to combat the problems of rural poor through its CMGs. Chitradurga district is characterised by frequent droughts and poor performance in both agricultural and industrial sectors. A large proportion of agricultural labourers in the district find it difficult to get employment all through the year. A large chunk of population is below the poverty line. Of them, most belong to SCs/STs, and suffer from problems of high illiteracy, more dependency on local moneylenders for their credit needs, etc. This, together with the failure of the government in providing better living conditions to the poor, motivated some of the like-minded social activists to make an organised effort to ameliorate the situation by starting GRAMA.

AREA OF OPERATION AND STAFF

The head office of GRAMA is located in Chitradurga, while the project office is at Challakere which is 60 kms. away from the district headquarters. The service area of GRAMA is largely concentrated in Challakere taluk (89 villages), Hiriyur (24 villages) and Chitradurga (23 villages), covering altogether 136 villages in Chitradurga district. Moreover, from 1997 onwards, GRAMA has extended its activities to Tumkur, Karwar and Hassan districts in Karnataka.

GRAMA has a total staff of 30, of whom 5 are administrators (3 men and 2 women) and 25 are field-workers (12 men and 13 women). At the grass roots level, women animators working under the control of hobli coordinators are the link between field staff and target group members. The decisions on the proposal, budget, programme development, policy formulation, implementation and monitoring of the programmes are prepared with the active participation of all the staff members of GRAMA.

TARGET GROUP OF GRAMA

GRAMA has identified rural women as its main target group who will be the prime movers of sustainable rural development process in the future. Most rural women are illiterates, unorganised, economically weak, become worst victims of discrimination, wife-beating, harassment, subordination, subjugation, etc., and completely neglected in decision-making, planning, implementation and monitoring the rural development programmes which are meant for them. In this situation, it is necessary that these women are motivated and involved in improving their own living conditions and brought into the mainstream of sustainable rural development through formation and promotion of CMGs. As a consequence, the people's institutions are formed mainly among the poor women. These people's institutions are seen as vehicles for accessing credit available within the government agencies seeking to improve the income generating potential of the poor, especially women.

The number of villages covered under the project has increased from 40 in 1996 to 136 in 1998. Similarly, the number of SHGs has also gone up to 309 from 160 during the same period (Table 11.1).

Table 11.1: Villages and target groups under GRAMA

Year	*No. of Villages*	*No. of groups*			*Target group members*		
		Male	*Female*	*Total*	*Male*	*Female*	*Total*
1996	40	—	160	160	—	3,153	3,153
1997	90	3	204	207	45	3,835	3,880
1998	136	3*	306	309	45	4,771	4,816

Note: *The group of men formed under the watershed development programme.

MAIN ACTIVITIES AND FUNDING SOURCES OF THE ORGANISATION

Income generation programmes through formation of CMGs

The formation of CMGs through which SHGs can ultimately be constituted has become the entry point of GRAMA. The CMGs are formed to bring the target members together on a single platform which will cater to the micro-credit needs and also address the felt needs and immediate day-to-day problems of the poor. The members are motivated to save and utilise the loan, and thereby linked with formal banking institutions. In order to ensure economic empowerment of the women, GRAMA has initiated micro finance and income generating activities providing loans from out of the group savings and/or from out of resources mobilised from the government.

Human Resources Development Programme

The organisation states that lack of education, skills, awareness, and poor health status, etc., have a bearing on rural poverty. Hence, emphasis has been given to the activities of providing adult education to SHG members, (i.e., numeracy and signature), providing non-formal education to school drop-outs and supplementary education for school-going children, and conducting education awareness camps for the public with regard to the importance of sending their children to school.

The organisation also believes that only when the poor are healthy could they work and eke out the required sustenance. With a view to improving their health status, it conducts awareness camps on health, health education, health training programmes and check-up camps. These activities also aim to activate the health departments towards delivering better health services to the rural masses.

Conservation and management of natural resources

The third important activity of the organisation is the conservation and management of natural resources to ensure sustainable agricultural development. Under this programme, preventing soil erosion, harvesting run-off water through watershed development programmes and plantation are the important activities. It also conducts some training programmes on the concept and awareness of joint forest management, integrated watershed development, natural resource conservation and management and utilisation and seed conservation.

SOURCE OF FUNDING

The funding to undertake these activities comes from both government and donor agencies. In 1991, GRAMA came into contact with NOVIB, a Netherlands based donor agency, and submitted a proposal for conducting a socio-economic survey and activities relating to providing awareness and forming SHGs etc. NOVIB initially provided funds for one year. Soon after the completion of the first phase, NOVIB considered GRAMA as a regular partner NGO to initiate the development activities in Chitradurga district. Since then NOVIB has been supporting the organisation for various developmental activities in terms of finance and guidance, etc., and has become the sole external funding agency.

Table 11.2 presents the quantum of funding from different sources in 1998 and fund allocation for several activities from NOVIB during 1996-1998.

Table 11.2: Quantum of funding to GRAMA *(In Rupees)*

Year	Name of the agency			
	Govt.	*Donor (NOVIB)*	*Self (GRAMA)*	*Total funding*
1996	813,500 (16.57)	3,521,766 (71.75)	573,321 (11.65)	4,908,587 (100)
1997	391,000 (8.16)	3,464,587 (72.32)	935,081 (19.52)	4,790,668 (100)
1998	1,373,000 (18.71)	4,031,581 (54.95)	1,932,811 (26.34)	7,337,392 (100)

Note: The figures in parentheses indicate percentages.

Though the donor agency provides larger proportions of funds for various activities, there is a gradual shift towards mobilising the resources from the government. However, NOVIB has fostered and developed GRAMA. The donor agency has been playing an important role in providing financial support, guidance and moral support in decision-making, monitoring, implementation of its various socio-economic activities in the region.

INTERFACE WITH GOVERNMENT AGENCIES

As per the understanding of the organisation, the interface is something in which the organisation can enable its target group members to approach and access the government resources on their own and involve themselves in planning, implementation and monitoring of the accessed programmes and making the interface sustainable.

GRAMA opines that despite the government's anti-poverty programmes, there is not much improvement in the living conditions of the rural poor. Even then, new programmes are being launched without considering the lacunae of the existing programmes, the feasibility of the programmes to be initiated and prerequisites for the programmes to become successful. It is in this context that GRAMA started to work with the government agencies to ensure that the government benefits reach the poor and improve their living conditions. While the overall aims and objectives of GRAMA and the government towards rural development are almost the same, the approaches and strategies to tackle the problems are different. The government, realising its inability to implement poverty alleviation programmes successfully through line departments, have started to involve the NGOs in delivering development programmes which are being implemented by the organisations. One such programme is

Rashtriya Mahila Kosh (RMK) which has been in operation across the country through the NGOs.

For the income generating activities to become sustainable, heavy capital investment and supportive infra-structural facilities at the grass roots level are required. GRAMA finds it difficult to mobilise funds out of group savings or motivate NOVIB to initiate several socio-economic activities through its CMGs. Therefore, the interface with the government departments becomes necessary to access and meet the ever increasing requirements of the rural poor.

LINKAGES

The following factors contribute to the process of facilitating linkages between various government departments and its target members:

- Most of the development programmes, implemented directly through government departments, have not really benefited the poor. The scarce resources are being syphoned off by the relatively better off. Hence, there is need to distribute the benefits to the poor through independent people's institutions.
- If the people are not motivated and organised, the resources available with the government for the betterment of rural poor, especially women are likely to be exploited by someone else. This is something which GRAMA does not wish to happen. Therefore, in order to utilise the resources, GRAMA is anxious to negotiate and establish good linkages with the government agencies.
- In order to ensure the sustainability of people's institutions and the programmes implemented, the linkages become inevitable. GRAMA, in future, may adopt the "Withdrawal Strategy" wherein the people's institutions have to sustain on their own. Unless they are able to establish sustained linkages with government departments, the withdrawal may not be possible.
- In view of ever increasing needs of the poor, the funds out of group savings and from donor agencies most often tend to become insufficient. Therefore, to meet such increased requirements of the poor, the linkages with the government departments become the need of the hour.

- In future, GRAMA wants to reduce its dependency on the donor agency and sustain on its own. To the extent possible, the resources are needed to be mobilised from the government.
- Moreover, the policies of the government, at times may not fulfil the needs of the poor and, therefore, many a poor are deprived of the facilities offered by the government. In order to influence the government policies in favour of the poor and the poorest, critical collaboration is very much needed.

Perception on linkages

Though GRAMA started establishing linkages with various line departments, it has pinpointed the need for building up linkages and strengthening the sustainability of the people's institutions and programmes. In view of this, GRAMA has succeeded in establishing critical linkages with the Department of Women and Child Development, HRD, Government of India, New Delhi, in accessing the RMK programme. As per the understanding of GRAMA on linkages, it is a forum in which the organisation can influence the government policies, programmes, and its process and initiation of the programmes in favour of the poor and downtrodden.

CENTRAL AND LOCAL GOVERNMENT PROGRAMMES

As noted in the previous sections, the organisation has established linkages with the central and state governments and has succeeded in accessing the programmes such as RMK (1994), SHGs linked NABARD-IG programme (1994) (Table 11.3)

Table 11.3: Government programmes accessed

Year	*Name of the programme*	*Central/ Local Govt.*	*Number of villages covered*	*Number of households benefited*	*Total assistance Rs.*
1996	RMK	Central Govt.	38	345	692,500
	NABARD	Central Govt.	16	77	187,000
	DWCRA	Local Govt.	2	20	30,000
1997	NABARD	Central Govt.	3	22	138,000
	DWCRA	Local Govt.	1	10	250,000
1998	RMK	Central Govt.	42	364	1,000,000
	NABARD	Central Govt.	14	84	397,000

Contributing factors

The following factors have influenced both the government and the organisation to provide and access the government programmes:

- Presenting the growth and progress of SHGs undertaking income generating activities in the meetings and workshops organised by the government departments have influenced the government officials to seek proper channels through which some of the government programmes can be implemented and monitored successfully.
- Commitment, dedication and involvement of the organisation in the removal of deep-rooted poverty and unemployment have made the governments to extend their support.
- Progress and performance of the people's institutions (SHGs) have attracted both the central and local governments to coordinate, cooperate and collaborate with the organisation for the sustainability of the programmes.
- Popularity of GRAMA may have influenced the line departments to take note of the aims and objectives of the organisation. As the aims and objectives of the organisation and government seem to overlap, both the actors have come together to work for the betterment of the poor.

Strategies adopted

The organisation has been successful in accessing the government programmes such as RMK, NABARD-IGP and DWCRA from both the central and local governments. The following strategies helped in accessing the government resources.

- Frequent conduct of meetings, workshops, awareness camps with the participation of the government officials.
- Attending the meetings and workshops organised by the government departments and presenting them the growth and progress of SHGs.
- Keeping constant contacts and good rapport building with the various line departments, and not bowing down to them.
- Making the aims and objectives of the organisation known to the government departments and motivating them to extend their helping hand.

- Encouraging the target group member to participate in the Panchayat Raj institutions (PRIs).[2]

Problems in the linkages process

The organisation faced problems while establishing linkages with the government organisation. An example to highlight the point is given below. The SHGs were not allowed to open the account in the bank. The bank officials did not have conceptual clarity of SHGs. Therefore, SHGs were not permitted to open the account in the first 2-3 months.

This compelled GRAMA to adopt the following strategies to establish linkages with the Banks: (*i*) writing letters to the Regional Office of NABARD and concerned lead bank with the aims and objectives of GRAMA; (*ii*) frequent meetings and negotiation with the Bank managers and explaining them the overall objectives of GRAMA; and (*iii*) meetings of SHGs were held for clarifying the objectives of the programme and the banks were persuaded to permit the target group to open the account. This could have perhaps influenced the NABARD to sanction IGP loan to the SHGs through the Chitradurga Grameena Bank. Since then the bank has been showing a positive and pro-active response towards the progress and growth of SHGs.

Perception of the target group members

To understand the perception of the target group on the interface, 20 women SHG members from four villages were interviewed. Of them, ten had obtained RMK loan, five NABARD loan and the rest had benefited from DWCRA programme. The sample members belong to the scheduled caste, scheduled tribe and other backward castes; most of them were landless and marginal households involved in one or other income generating activities (Table 11.4).

Table 11.4 : Distribution of sample members

	Size of landholdings (%)					
Caste group/size class	*Landless*	*Marginal*	*Small*	*Medium*	*Large*	*Total*
Scheduled Castes	25	10	—	—	—	35
Scheduled Tribes	5	—	5	—	—	10
Other backward castes	10	10	25	5	5	55
Total	40	20	30	5	5	100
Actuals	(8)	(4)	(6)	(1)	(1)	(20)

To obtain information relating to various government programmes, a large proportion of the sample members depended on GRAMA, school teachers, gram panchayat staff, and other government village level officials. For all of them, GRAMA was the main source of information, awareness and guidance for almost all the on-going developmental programmes. Further, it might be recorded that GRAMA was perhaps providing information on government sponsored poverty alleviation programmes such as RMK, DWCRA, NABARD-IGP, IRDP loans, sanitary and latrine schemes, bhagya jyothi and community development schemes such as drainage, water facility, street light, road laying and repairs while the rest were probably providing information on the areas in which they were involved.

A majority of the sample members were aware of the IRDP, loans to OAP, handicapped and Bhagyajyothi, loans for agriculture, sanitary facilities, NABARD-IGP and RMK. (Table 11.5).

A large proportion of the sample respondents had been able to apply for obtaining the programmes but a very few of them succeeded in accessing the programmes such as RMK, loans to rural artisans, loans to OAP, handicapped, Bhagyajyothi, loans to sanitary facilities, etc. The utilisation of the programmes accessed was not up to the mark (Table 11.5).

Table 11.5 : Programmes aware of, applied for, accessed and productively utilised

Programmes	*Percentage of members*			
	Programmes aware of	*Programmes applied for*	*Programmes obtained*	*Productive use of programmes*
NABARD-IGP	55	40	25	—
IRD Programme	80	55	25	—
Rastriya Mahila Kosh	50	50	50	30
DWCRA	30	30	25	20
Loans to rural artisans	35	30	30	30
Loans to agriculture	59	10	10	—
Loans to OAP, handicapped and Bhagyajyothi	70	59	30	30
Loans to sanitary facilities	55	40	25	—
SC/ST Corporation Scheme	5	5	—	—

A little less than half of the sample respondents did not face any problems in accessing the government programmes as there was an animator who took care of the whole process of writing and filling up the applications, submitting it and its timely follow-up. However, the problem of frequent visits to meet them, coming out, speaking to the government officials, inordinate delay in sanctioning the loan amount, mobilising the necessary documents, red tapism etc., were faced by the rest of the sample members (Table 11.6).

Table 11.6 : Problems faced in establishing linkages with government departments

Particulars	*Total no. of respondents*	*Percentage*
Writing the application	2	10
Speaking to govt. officials	5	25
No problem faced as there were Animators	9	45
Mobilising some requirements	2	10
Frequent visits and meeting the officials	9	45
Sharing the accessed loan amount	1	5
Inordinate delay in sanctioning the loan	3	15

Most of the sample beneficiaries depended on GRAMA for approaching and accessing the government benefits. However, a few of the sample members also depended on anganwadi teachers, school teachers, bank officials, gram panchayat officials, and nurses to obtain certain benefits from the government which were available with the above said officials. Nevertheless, it is to be noted that GRAMA played an important role in motivating, facilitating and making them access and obtain most of the benefits from the government (Table 11.7).

Table 11.7 : Economic impact of the programme

Particulars		*Total number of respondents*	*Average*
Units not in productive use		6	—
Units in gestation period to yield income		3	—
Units in productive use (UPU) as of now		11	—
Number of persons involved in UPU		18	—
Capital invested	Rs.	70,500	6,409
Loan obtained	Rs.	52,000	4,727
Turnover	Rs.	46,955	4,269
Variable cost	Rs.	33,636	3,058
Margins per person	Rs.	13,319	25

A large proportion of the sample members who obtained income generation programmes had productively utilised them for both income and employment generation and very few of them had used the loan amount as working capital for woollen weaving activity and some of them had used it for marriage purpose, educating their children and meeting their immediate domestic expenses. Every sample member who was productively involved in the activity got around Rs. 740 per month so that everyone earned Rs. 25 per day from the income generating activities (Tables 11.7 and 11.8).

Table 11.8: Utilisation of the accessed programmes

Particulars	*Total no. of respondents*	*Percentage*
Income	4	20
Employment	2	10
Income and employment	6	30
Working capital	2	10
Unproductive use	6	30
Total	20	100

As regards repayment of the loan obtained, less than half of the sample beneficiaries had been able to repay the loan amount without any overdue; more so, in the case of RMK programme followed by NABARD-IGP. A less proportion of the sample members was also found to have made repayment with overdues in RMK programme. Out of 20 sample beneficiaries, 5 had repaid the loan amount with overdues and another 5 had partially repaid without overdues. (Table 11.9).

Table 11.9: Repayment of loans by schemes

Particulars	*RMK*	*IGP*	*DWCRA*	*Total*
Repaid without overdues	62.5	25	12.5	40
Repaid with overdues	80	—	20	25
Did not repay at all	—	—	100	5
Partially repaid with overdues	—	100	—	5
Partially repaid without overdues	20	40	40	25
Total	50	25	25	100

A majority of the sample members who had experience in obtaining the government programmes were not confident of approaching the government officials on their own to access the resources in the future. However, 5 out of 20 were independent in approaching and accessing the benefits from the government. And, four of them are still fully dependent on GRAMA and the remaining 4 needed initial support (Table 11.10).

Table 11.10: Approaching the government officials

Particulars	*Total no. of respondents*	*Percentage*
Not confident in approaching on their own	7	35
Independent in approach	5	25
Fully dependent on GRAMA	4	20
Dependent for initiating the process and afterwards no need	4	20
Total	20	100

CONCLUSION

It is clear from the foregoing discussion that GRAMA firmly believes that key to alleviate deep-rooted poverty and unemployment lies in social, economical and political empowerment of the weaker sections of the society. Accordingly, GRAMA has been marching towards ensuring empowerment of the weaker sections especially the poor women with a set of activities addressing different issues to build up sustainable people's institutions so that these people's institutions are able to put forth their needs and access resources from the government. GRAMA perceives that the linkages with the government are needed to enable the poor to access the resources, and influence policies in favour of the poor. GRAMA mobilised resources from various government agencies, and the impact of these resources on the poor is positive. The organisation sees the interface process as enabling the poor to access the resources on their own from the government. But, the primary data shows that most of the members are still not independent in approaching the government agencies. This is an area which needs to be concentrated in the future.

NOTES

1. GRAMA was registered as a trust on 12th July 1989. It started functioning only in 1990 with Mrs. Girijamma Rudraiah as chief functionary. She has vast experience of social work in the rural areas.
2. The organisation facilitated the process of target group members to enter into gram panchayats. Altogether 14 target group members contested and won in the election held in 1995.

12

NGOs and Government Agencies

Experiences of Dale View

CHRISTU DAS & P. SHOBANA

INTRODUCTION

Dale View began its work as a charity organisation in Punalal of Thiruvananthapuram district in Kerala State. It was registered as Punalal Mahila Samajam, a women`s organisation, in 1976. Initially, the focus of the organisation was to address the problems that existed at that time in the village, namely, illiteracy, illicit production of alcohol, exploitation of natural resources like trees, lack of market support for traditional business (bamboo basket weaving), absence of political organisation, etc. The entry point taken up to reach the people was a small nursery school, through which programmes like mid-day meal and food for nursing mothers were implemented. To obtain the support of villagers, sports activities were organised. Later, in 1978, the organisation extended its activities by registering as NGO called as Dale View, with a major focus on education and infrastructural development.

The overall objective of the organisation is to create a participatory interactive just society based on values inculcated through a process of education and capacity-building with a belief in and respect for the worth and capacity of human beings.

This objective is being achieved through various activities in areas like education, health, welfare, women's development, environment, agriculture, animal husbandry, rehabilitation, training, and vocational training. The major activities of the organisation are: education and training, micro-credit, housing and sanitation and deaddiction. These activities are being implemented in seven villages covering the target group members of 11,483 (Table 12.1).

Table 12.1: Villages and target groups

Year	*No. of villages*	*Total no. of target groups*	*Total target group population*
1996	5	256	8,560
1997	7	330	9,500
1998	7	336	11,483

Sources of funding

These activities are supported financially from different sources like Rashtriya Mahila Kosh (RMK), CAPART and Ministry of Social Welfare. The education programme is a self-supportive programme. Table 12.2 shows the sources of funding from government, donor and self.

Table 12.2: Sources of funding since 1995-96

(in Rupees)

Source/Year	*1995-96*	*1996-97*	*1997-98*
Government	2,171,938.2 (31.39)	3,960,480 (37.13)	4,387,876 (45.96)
Donor	1,632,625.9 (23.60)	3,230,793 (30.30)	1,515,070 (15.87)
Self	3,114,528.6 (45.02)	3,474,935 (32.58)	3,644,448 (38.17)
Total	6,919,092.7 (100)	10,666,208 (100)	9,547,394 (100)

Note: *The figures in the parentheses are column-wise percentages.

The funding from the donor agency has reduced during the period 1995-96 to 1997-98 while that of the government has increased. The decrease in the donor funding is not because of any problem, but the donor cannot support any NGO for a long time on a sustained basis. The donor agencies normally support an organisation for a period of time for it to become self-sustained. This is true in the case of Dale View as well. The gradual decrease in the funding from donor agencies has partly contributed to the interface with the government.

The NGO has a number of staff members who are instrumental in implementing the programmes. Micro-credit programme has 361 animation supervisors, volunteers and clerical staff. For undertaking the activities of education and deaddiction centre, there are 114 staff members. Micro-credit programme is one of the major programmes of the organisation in terms of the size of funding and the number of staff.

Interface with government agencies

The organisation is mobilising government resources and this has facilitated the linkage between various central government departments and target group members. The linkage with the government agencies is mainly because the government has a number of programmes specifically for the poor, and the poor are entitled to avail the programme. Also, the ideology of the government schemes and that of the NGO are congruent. As the government resources are to be channelised to the poor, and given the inability of the bureaucracy to effectively implement the programmes, the NGO fills the gap towards reaching the poor. In a sense, the NGO acts as an extended hand of the government.

The interface becomes all the more important as the government is incapable of identifying the right beneficiary and monitor the process. The NGOs interfacing with the government fill these gaps and also help the people reach the government. The NGO has been successful in mobilising government resources. It mobilised Rs. 21.72 lakhs in 1995-96, Rs. 37.90 lakhs in 1996-97 and Rs. 43.88 lakhs in 1997-98 (Table 12.3).

Table 12.3: Funds (in Rs.) mobilised from various departments during 1996-98

Source	*1995-96*	*1996-97*	*1997-98*
CAPART	1,102,404	2,938,731	2,246,903
Ministry of Social Welfare	1,050,884	851,363	844,110
KSSWAB	18,480	–	18,480
SIDBI	–	–	22,470
RMK	–	–	1,100,000
District Panchayat	–	–	156,000
Total	2,171,768	3,790,094	4,387,963

The strategies adopted by the NGO in mobilising these programmes are explained in brief below:

- While meeting the government officials for funding, the NGO goes well prepared with all the needed documents and also backed up with the needed experience. For instance, when the Rashtriya Mahila Kosh, New Delhi, had called for a meeting of all the NGOs in Kerala, the Dale View attended the meeting. The Dale View presented its organisational activities with the experience in micro-credit and also presented the records which showed all the savings and credits of its members. This was very impressive, and the RMK officials chose the Dale View for inspection.
- Inviting officials for inspection even before the sanction of the programmes so as to provide the officials with better understanding of the programmes.
- Opening opportunities for officials to meet with the target group members of the village.
- Regular follow-up of the process with utmost patience. For instance, the CAPART programme on housing was sanctioned for 344 houses in 1987 while the money was released only in 1991. The delay was handled patiently with regular follow-up through letters and occasional visit to the CAPART office at New Delhi. During the subsequent phase (1995-98), the funds were released within a period of 6-8 months which helped to construct 344 houses during this period. Thus, the regular follow-up yie!ded in 'quick' release during the second phase.
- Acceptance of certain obligations of the government, like the IAS officers undergoing training in their organisation (a training mandatory for the IAS officers), and using their training centre for conducting government training programmes.
- Productive utilisation of the earlier programmes and the sincerity of the same have also contributed for the linkage.
- Use of participatory techniques in the identification of the needs of the people and implementation of the programmes.
- Directly approaching the concerned officials.

Adopting these strategies the NGO has not only succeeded many a time in mobilising the resources but has also experienced failures. They have also faced some problems, difficulties and constraints in accessing the government programmes. They are :

- Delay in timely release of the funds to implement the project subsequently lead to the delay in the completion of the assignment.
- Frequent transfer of officials delayed the process. Establishing rapport with the present officials is an additional problem of delay.
- Most of the rules of the government lack flexibility which comes in the way of successful implementation of the programme. For instance, the RMK sanctions the second phase of funding only on the cent per cent recovery of the first loan amount. But due to natural calamities the beneficiaries incurred losses in their business and failed to repay the first obtained loans. The failure in the repayment delays the sanction of the second loan which has a negative impact on those who are in real need of the credit facility.
- The indifference of the officials in responding in the right way with the NGO. The Dale View submitted a proposal to the CAPART for the construction of open wells in 1994. After regular follow-up of the proposal the response from the office was that the particular file was missing which also meant the rejection of the proposal. This indifferent response from the government came after a period of one year.
- The NGO has certain limitations. Sometimes the proposals submitted to the government were not up to the expectation and the NGO had realised this fact. But these proposals had been summarily rejected by the government officials without even discussion with the NGO.

The NGO encouraged its target group members to participate in the panchayat elections. Awareness programmes and training programmes were conducted in the SHG meetings. Ten of the target group members won the panchayat elections, of whom one won the office of President of the Panchayat. Among the ten, eight were women and two were men.

The Dale View has many networks at the district, state and national levels. The networks are programme specific. There are networks exclusively for deaddiction, micro-credit, etc. The notable and functioning networks are KELNET (Kerala Network) and INNET (India Network) which function for the micro-credit programmes. They also work on the lobbying for changes in certain government policies regarding micro-credit programme. INNET has members all over the country while KELNET is a budding network which has members from the state of Kerala. The NGO perceives networking as a channel for creating positive impact on policy making. However, the government agencies implemented the programme through the officials of various departments without taking the network and its members into consideration. This resulted in wrong implementation of the programmes by the government. In spite of this, Dale View is still looking forward to influence the government machinery by abstaining from bribes, favouritism or sectarian mentality, etc.

To effectively deal with the problems in obtaining the government programmes, to cross the unwanted but inevitable hurdles and tactfully handle the loopholes and malpractices of the government, the Dale View finds that the target group members in the decentralised government body are ineffective. Though the NGO has given awareness training on the Panchayat Raj Institutions for its target group members, its actual involvement is not much.

Perceptions of the target group members

The perceptions of twenty target group members were obtained on the linkage with the government by canvassing a questionnaire among them. The sample members were the beneficiaries of the RMK programme and the CAPART housing programme. They belonged to two villages, Changa and Valliyanur. The criteria for selecting the sample members were that they should belong to the above said village and should be beneficiaries of the mentioned government programmes.

The sample members were aware of programmes, such as housing, sanitation, TRYSEM, DWCRA, PMRY, national maternity benefit scheme, RMK, IRDP, PDS, SIDBI, drinking water, agricultural training programmes, Krishi Bhavan Scheme (scheme for crop loans through agricultural department) and free electricity facility. A majority of the sample members were aware of housing, IRDP, Krishi Bhavan, and sanitation programmes while the rest of the programme were known by only a few. Most of the sample members had applied for RMK and housing programme and had been successful in availing them. Table 12.4 shows the level of awareness of the sample members about the government programmes, and also provides information as proportion of members applying and availing the schemes.

None of the sample members met any government official to avail the programme. All the programmes were channelled through the NGO. Hence, most of the sample members did not have any problem, difficulties or constraints in availing the benefit, while a few had certain difficulties because of the delay in the process.

Table 12.4: Level of awareness of the sample members

Government programmes	*Percentage of members*		
	Aware	*Applied*	*Availed*
Housing	90	50	50
RMK	50	50	50
Sanitation	50	10	10
IRDP	75	10	10
Krishi Bhavan scheme	60	15	–
PMRY	45	–	–
Drinking water	40	15	10
PDS	10	10	10
TRYSEM	15	–	–
Free electricity facility	5	5	5

The process of availing the government programme was followed up at different offices. Some of them had followed up at the SHG, while some at the NGO and a few at both the places. But none of them visited the government office for any follow-up.

Table 12.5: Approaching the government departments

Particulars	*No. of respondents*	*Percentage*
Can approach independently	9	45
Needs support of Dale View and SHG	4	20
Fully dependent on Dale View and SHG	7	35
Total	20	100

To establish the linkage with the government department and to avail the benefit, all the sample members had depended upon the NGO. None of the sample members had paid bribe to anyone in the process of availing the benefit.

The availed government programme has created some impact on the household. All the sample members who availed the housing programme of CAPART had utilised the benefit in constructing a house and are living in the newly constructed houses. Among the sample members who had availed RMK loans, only one had not productively utilised while the rest had increased their income by productively utilising the loan benefit. A majority of the sample members who had got the loans have repaid it. A majority of the sample members who had availed the CAPART programme had come to know of the programme through the villagers while only a few knew the programme through the NGO. All the sample members who had availed the RMK benefit knew the programme through the SHG.

A majority of the sample members considered the NGO as provider and helper in accessing the programme, while a few considered it as a bridge and agent between the government and the target group.

The sample members were in a position to approach the government officials independently, but needed the backing up of the NGO or SHG. Some were fully dependent on the NGO.

CONCLUSION

Though the NGO has some self-financing programmes, it still depends on government and donor funds to cater to the larger needs of the people of that region. The organisation has been mobilising the government resources as it perceives that they are due to the people.

They have been successful in accessing the resources from CAPART for more than 10 years and from RMK for about five years. This success is mainly because of the productive and sincere utilisation of the resources. The organisation has faced problems of rejection and delay in the sanction of many projects that it had proposed. Despite this, the Dale View is making a continuous effort to mobilise the resources. The level of dependence of the target group on NGO is still high. The NGO aims to take up the role of a facilitator and catalyst for the people to access the government resources by building their capacities so that the people can directly interface with the government department to get their needs fulfilled. The Dale View strongly believes that this mode of operation is more effectively successful and above all sustainable.

13

Interface with Government Agencies

Experiences of SHARE

K. MURUGESAN & P. SHOBANA

INTRODUCTION

Self-help Association for Rural Education and Employment (SHARE) is a grass roots level organisation founded in 1991. Since its inception, it is involved in multifaceted and integrated development aimed at women's empowerment in the rural areas of Vellore District, Tamil Nadu. The main strengths of the organisation are in the domain of income generation, skill development and self-help promotion. SHARE is, by and large, an organisation for women, and participants in the various projects are rural women. During the seven years of its existence, SHARE has been able to establish and maintain effective linkages with other NGOs[1], and central and state government agencies. The experience gained in the process of establishing linkages, the factors that contributed to the linkages and also those which discouraged the interface process have been presented in this chapter.

About the organisation

SHARE is mainly an organisation of the women, for the women and by the women in so far as all its members are women, and all the programmes are for women. Planning, implementation, monitoring and evaluation are done by the women.

SHARE had its genesis with the formation of a women's society called Edayan Sathu Women Movement. This was initiated by a doctor, Dr. Christine Mathews from CMC, who was interested in the health of the people and who had realised that economic development is a prerequisite for the people to utilise the existing health delivery system. Hence, craft activities in palm leaf products, fibre knitting and carpet making were introduced. The organisation was registered under the name of SHARE.

Objectives of SHARE

The main objective of SHARE is the economic empowerment of rural women. The specific objectives of SHARE are to : (*i*) organise, educate and motivate women to take up gainful occupation so that they can have supplementary income and thereby improve their image in the family and society; (*ii*) progressively improve working skills and enhance their economic status so that women are able to make decisions at household and community levels; (*iii*) create awareness among women on various issues relating to suppression of women in rural areas, and to make them knowledgeable about the rights of women envisaged in the Constitution; (*iv*) build the capacity of the women in economic, social, and political spheres; (*v*) mobilize the government programmes that are meant for the development of individuals and communities; and, (*vi*) promote self-help concept among women.

Legally, SHARE can carry out its activities all over Tamil Nadu. But, SHARE concentrates its activities in two districts, viz., Vellore and Thiruvannamalai. The NGO is covering 50 villages in the blocks of Kaniyambadi, Anaicut, Vellore and Jawadi Hills, and works for the rural poor women and children with special emphasis on the *dalits*, tribals and the poor among the backward and most backward castes. The NGO has seven staff members in the administration and 19 staff at the programme level.

Important activities of SHARE

Among several of the socio-economic, educational, political and cultural activities that SHARE has undertaken, the following three need special mention:

- Organisation of skill training and skill development programmes for women with an in-built mechanism to enable the skilled women to start production units with provision for marketing help.
- Organisation of need-based awareness building and education programmes on gender issues, participation in the local decentralised government, alternative education for children, etc.
- Propagation of the principles and usefulness of self-help, organisation of self-help groups and giving encouragement to self-help promotional activities.

Sources of funding

In 1991, when SHARE was established, the funds for the NGO came entirely from its own sources. The reason for this non-dependence on external funding was because the NGO was undertaking only craft activity which provided some surplus income to the NGO, and no other development activity which required funding. In 1993-94, the Development Commissioner for Handicrafts (DCH) provided funds for skill development. The NGO obtained funding from external donor agency (GTZ/SHF) only in 1995. The details of the funding during 1997-98 are provided in Table 13.1.

Table 13.1: Funding by sources during 1997-98

Source of funding	*Amount (Rs.)*
Government	227,682 (5)
Donor	833,793 (19)
Self	3,279,652 (76)
Total	4,341,127 (100)

Note: The figures in parentheses are percentages to the total funding.

The following are the problems faced with external donors according to SHARE.

- The donors do not consider the needs of the people/ community. Their funding is based on their policies and budget.
- Delay in fund allocation: The funds are so delayed that the cost goes up and funds become insufficient.

- Funding is not based on performance. The deserving NGO is kept away from the funds.
- Donors promise certain funds, ultimately, do not provide the same by stating some reasons (Box 13.1).
- Without understanding the NGO objectives, the donors insist on changes that may go against the NGO objectives (Box 13.2).

Box 13.1: An experience with GTZ/SHF
GTZ/SHF promised to provide part of the funds required for the construction of a building provided SHARE mobilised the remaining funds from the government. Hoping to receive the fund from GTZ/SHF, SHARE mobilised Rs. 640,000 from the government. The funds were released to SHARE, the only NGO to have obtained government assistance for constructing a building in Vellore district. Later, GTZ/SHF refused to fund the building. SHARE could neither construct the building with the amount sanctioned by the government nor could it refuse, because if the organisation did so, the money would have gone forever, and the future linkages would have become difficult. SHARE is now in a dilemma.

Box 13.2: An experience with PHP
PHP is a donor agency from the USA. SHARE approached the PHP for funds for dairy farming which was agreed to initially. But, later, the donor recommended a different design for the project which was not appealing to SHARE. Hence refrained from making further progress. Subsequently, PHP came up with some changes in the design which SHARE was willing to adopt. Such pressure from a donor is uncomfortable to the organisation.

Perception on interface with government agencies

According to SHARE, interface linkages with the government agencies is to tap the resources that are due for the people. NGOs should not work as distribution centres of the government resources and programmes. They should take up the responsibility to empower the people so that they can establish the linkage and the NGO should play only passive role in mobilising the resources. The process of empowering, establishing linkage and mobilizing the resources is referred to as interface by SHARE. The empowerment should provide the awareness on the government benefit and/or resources to the poor, educate them on their ownership towards the programmes and finally the ways to tap the resources. These resources may or may not be mobilised with the support of the NGO; but, the NGOs should certainly perform the role of a catalyst in the process. They should monitor the follow-up system that was created by the people.

As noted earlier, SHARE began development work with resources mobilised from its own craft activity. The functioning of craft activity is as follows: After providing skills to women members, the organisation supplies raw materials to them, who produce palm leaf products. The products are collected and marketed by SHARE in the international and national markets. SHARE passes on the earnings to meet the salaries of staff, office and administration expenses, and also to initiate development activities such as giving scholarships to girl children. As such, the organisation could have managed to undertake development activities with earnings from craft activity, but, the needs of members have continuously increased. Some of the felt needs of the members were training in advanced skills, capital for income generation activities, support facilities such as creches, drinking water, etc. The NGO has found it difficult to meet these needs from earnings of craft activity. Hence, it started to access funds from both external donors and government agencies.

Linkages with government agencies

The important factors contributing to linkages between government agencies and SHARE can be summed up as follows:

- To fulfil the objectives of the SHARE, it is necessary and inevitable to establish linkages with government agencies so that it can tap all the available resources. This is especially because the NGO does not have a broad financial base of its own.
- The objective set forth by the government in launching several of its poverty alleviation and social welfare programmes are very similar to the objectives of SHARE. Therefore, SHARE believes that it stands to gain if it can cooperate, coordinate and collaborate with the government agencies in programmes and activities meant for the poor and downtrodden.

- It is the experience of the NGO that funds allocated by the government for development of women are unused due to lack of organisations among women, lack of credible NGO, lack of suitable proposals, etc. An example is funds allocated for TRYSEM training. In order to utilise the dormant funds, SHARE actively seeks to establish linkages with government agencies.
- For reasons mentioned earlier, SHARE wants to reduce its dependence on external donors. Hence, resources are mobilised from the government.

Central government programmes

Within 2 years of its formation, SHARE was able to establish linkages with central government agencies. An Advanced Skill Training Programme in Palm leaf and Fibre was sanctioned by the Development Commissioner, Handicrafts, for the benefit of 30 women. Since then, SHARE has been maintaining the established linkages successfully intact over the year (Table 13.2).

Table 13.2: Programme accessed from the central government

Year	*Programmes*	*No. of house-holds benefited*	*Total amount received (Rs. in lakhs)*
1993-94	Advanced skill training programme	30	1.2
1994-95	Setting up of craft development centres	682	7.5
1994-1997	Market meet & product promotion programme	SHARE	0.5
1994-1997	Craft bazaar/Exhibitions	SHARE	1.5

Factors contributing to linkages

The following factors have contributed to the establishment of linkages with the Office of the Development Commissioner (Handicrafts).

- The relationship with this agency was established in the beginning itself. The handicraft trade was the result of the initiation and support provided by the Department of Community Health, Christian Medical College, Vellore. The image of CHAD (with which SHARE collaborates very closely) as a reputed institution in the district, should have prompted the officials to come forward to extend their support and cooperation in its initial stages.

- In SHARE, the programmes sanctioned were implemented in such a way that the objectives stipulated were met to the maximum extent. This motivated the officials to provide continuous support.
- SHARE has demonstrated to all the concerned and other actors that here is an organisation where a genuine attempt is being made to allow women to participate and decide for themselves. In other words, SHARE has amply demonstrated that it is marching forward in accordance with the objective of empowering women.
- SHARE makes efforts to be courteous and hospitable to its visitors. The NGO is also quite respectful when making visits to government offices. This should have impressed the government officials.

Problems encountered

No serious problems were encountered in dealing with the above mentioned government agency. The officials, in general, were too willing to help SHARE. Nevertheless, the NGO faced problems that are routine to any agency in dealing with a government department. To mention a few:

- Bureaucratic attitude of some of the officials quite often lead to tarnishing the images of the good officers also.
- Delays between application and actual sanctioning, and also between sanction and actual release of funds, are common.
- Corrupt attitude of the officials. A strong and innate feeling that nothing in the government office moves without bribe has been a major hassle for SHARE to proceed with its work.
- For the sake of establishing good rapport and maintaining congenial relationship, one has to be careful in the use of language. The NGO is 'scared' about the kind of response it gets from the government officials notwithstanding the fact that they are aware that it is the duty of the officers to serve the people.

Despite these problems, SHARE places on record its indebtedness to the government agency for having made available the above mentioned programmes through which it has been able to develop infrastructure facilities, conduct craft development training programmes, and start market promotional activities.

Local government programmes

SHARE has also established linkages with local government agencies such as DRDA, Khadi and Village Industries Board (KVIB) and Nationalised Banks (Table 13.3).

Table 13.3: Details of programmes obtained from local government agencies

Name of the agency	*Programmes*	*Beneficiary*	*Villages*	*Funds (in lakhs)*
DRDA	TRYSEM	220	7	10.00
DRDA	DWCRA	330	22	5.50
DRDA	IRDP	60	11	3.00
Bank	Direct loans	50	5	2.50
Bank	SHARE	—	—	2.00
KVIB	Craft loans for artisans	110	3	1.26

SHARE has facilitated loans from banks and other promotional agencies for the community. These include the commercial and cooperative banks and Khadi and Village Industries Commission. The children of the study centres have promoted social forestry through the facilitation of SHARE. Sometimes the facilitation would be indirect in the sense that the community would be made aware of the government programmes of the different departments or venues which can be accessed for achieving their targets and needs through capacity building.

Views of the NGO on panchayat elections

SHARE views the participation of the target group members in panchayat as avenues for : (*i*) 'bombarding' the government; (*ii*) obtaining opportunities to monitor panchayat programmes; (*iii*) mobilising and implementing need based programmes; (*iv*) acquiring knowledge on the functioning of the local administration; and (*v*) obtaining more power and authority for the people in implementing the programmes.

Accordingly, the organisation played a pro-active role in getting its members elected to gram panchayats. Altogether, 21 target women contested in the panchayat elections. Of them, three contested for panchayat president, one for councillor (town panchayat) and 17 for ward membership. Of them, nine won the election for ward membership; but none won the panchayat president's position.

In the last one year, SHARE has experienced success stories as well as unsuccessful stories (Box 13.3). But, the NGO has not lost hope in enabling the target group women to control decision-making on resources. It organises meetings among Panchayat members to pool information on the functioning of different panchayats in the block, and to take corrective measures, if any.

Box 13.3: Experiences of the TGMs as Panchayat members

Two of the target group members' experiences have been shared here. They are Ms. Poornima of Sholavaram village and Ms. Paun of Edayansathu village.

Ms. Poornima is a case of success. She has represented her village as ward member at the BDO and Collector's office and has implemented quite a few programmes of the government in the village. They are IRDP loans for six needy villagers, housing facilities, lighting facilities (Janatha light), laying of roads, etc.

Ms. Paun faces problems with the panchayat president in implementing the programmes of the government. The president, a woman candidate, hardly conducts or attends the meetings of gram panchayat. She doe not attend the meetings of government departments. Her husband takes over everything. Paun feels that the panchayat funds are simply wasted on unwanted programmes like construction of bridges (which is actually not needed) instead of construction of houses for the roofless. These kinds of activities are undertaken more often as the commission (from the contractor to the president) for the construction of bridges is more. But, Paun is still struggling to do good for her ward.

Contributing factors

In addition to the factors contributing to the maintenance of linkages with the central government agency, the following are important:

- As far as TRYSEM and DWCRA Programmes are concerned, the DRDA, on its own, approaches SHARE to implement these programmes in the targetted villages as the record of SHARE in undertaking, implementing and managing similar programmes has always been good over the years.

- SHARE has been able to earn goodwill and name among top level district officials including the collector as an agency truly working for the development of women and children. As a result, the former secretary of SHARE was accorded membership in the Governing Body of DRDA, which, in turn, provided ample opportunities to have linkages.
- SHARE is convinced that transparency plays an important role in building linkages with the government. SHARE provides room for the officials to directly interact with the people to cross-check the information given by the NGO. This has influenced the district level officials in taking a decision to work together.
- SHARE makes an attempt to participate in the government programmes and also involves the government officials in its programmes (Box 13.4).

Box 13.4: Willingness to participate in the government programmes

The government programme on the eradication of elephantiasis was taken up by the CMC. In this programme, mass vaccination for the people was organised. SHARE volunteered to participate in the programme. They participated by bringing awareness in the people about the need for vaccination and mobilise the people to get vaccinated during the camp.

The government had to implement a watershed programme in villages in four blocks of Vellore District. One of the components of the programme was self-help promotion. SHARE took up the responsibility of giving orientation on the concepts and the process of self-help to the beneficiaries of the programme in a 15-day training programme.

- The government machinery wants to experiment some programmes with NGOs which have the reputation of involving people in the development activities and which are sincere. According to government officials, SHARE has these qualities, and this is the only organisation which is genuinely community based and women-oriented organisation in the district. This has prompted the government to come forward to have linkages with SHARE.
- SHARE's style of functioning has also helped establish linkages. Its solidarity, sincerity, accountability, transparency and effective human resource development are added assets.

- SHARE offers good hospitality to all its visitors from the government departments, irrespective of the cadre to which they belong. They are attended to with a quick response, which has inspired the officials and has created a good impression.
- SHARE helps government officials in completing their targets. For example, the BDO of Kanniyambadi had to meet the target of mobilizing Rs. 3 Crores as recurring deposit from the people. To achieve this target, SHARE helped the BDO by giving the list of persons contributing recurring deposit from within the target group. By doing so, SHARE hoped to win the goodwill of the officials.
- SHARE is too willing to work with the government departments and also in sharing a few of their responsibilities. For example, the responsibility of the Collector to gather information on the viable income generating activities of the district was shared by the NGO. The animators of SHARE conducted a small study on the viable income generating activities in the Kanniyambadi block and the information was passed on to the Collector.
- SHARE has much success in establishing linkages. This could be because the representatives of the organisation are women and that they present the needs of the people very emotionally. An additional point to the credit of the NGO is that the NGO is run by women, who are considered as the vulnerable section of the community.
- SHARE adopts certain strategies depending on the situation (Box 13.5).

Box 13.5: Interesting strategies of SHARE

Thirty women had applied for TRYSEM training through SHARE to the Collector. The Collector was positive, but the BDO rejected the proposal. Given the reputation that the BDO was very corrupt, the women thought that he was rejecting because he was expecting a bribe. They thought of adopting three strategies: (*i*) give the bribe and report the same to the vigilance department; (*ii*) conduct the training without support from TRYSEM; and (*iii*) embarrass him by organising a march for sanctioning the programme, and by thanking him. They decided to adopt the third strategy. So, they arranged for a clandestine meeting where they planned to hold placards in praise of the BDO to embarrass him. This idea somehow reached the BDO and he rushed to the meeting place and immediately sanctioned the training to the applicants.

Problems faced

Some of the problems encountered with officials of the central government agency like administrative bureaucracy, red tapism etc. have also been encountered at the local level. Sanctioning to organisations which have no *locus standi* and which have no good record while rejecting the same to the genuine ones also has been experienced. However, the government officials have realised their mistake as they experienced problems with NGOs with poor record. This seems to have led the very same officials to come forward to request the SHARE to take up programmes which otherwise would have been directly implemented by them.

So far, NGO has not utilised the strategy of NGO network to mobilise the resources. In SHARE's perception, networking among NGOs should be genuine. All the NGOs who hold membership in the network should work for a common cause and should not articulate the personal needs while lobbying with the government departments. In order to attain such kind of cooperation among the networking NGOs, there should be homogeneity in the membership in terms of vision, style of functioning, etc.

SHARE is a part of the network called South India Producer's Association (SIPA). Through this network, lobbying on the Co-operative Act is done. The Government of India has made an attempt to draft a model Co-operative Act through a team of its staff who work in consultation with the NGOs. SHARE takes part in the preparation of the draft through the network. The network tries to bring out the incongruence in the democratic rules stated by the law and the reality. It also identifies the problems and/or the voids in the Act.

Perceptions of the target group members

Twenty women from three target villages of SHARE (Edayan Sathu, Kilpallipattu and Pennathur) were interviewed to fathom the perception of the target group. In these villages, SHARE has been working since its inception. The selection of the women was based on the criteria that they should be involved in any one of the important activities of SHARE and should be articulated. All the sample members were landless and marginal farmers belonging to SC and backward castes (Table 13.4).

Table 13.4: Distribution (%) of sample households

Caste group	*Landless farmers*	*Marginal farmers*	*Total* %	*Total* numbers
Backward Castes (BCs)	20	–	20	4
Most Backward Castes	10	20	30	6
Scheduled Castes (SCs)	40	10	50	10
Total	14	6	100	20

The sample members were aware of 18 government programmes in total. All of them were aware of Integrated Rural Development Programme (IRDP). They were, however, not aware of the programme by its name. In the discussions, the sample members referred the programme as the one which provided long-term loans for milch animals, poultry, petty shops, etc. A majority of the sample members were aware of the marriage grant given to the educated (8th class and beyond) brides belonging to the households below poverty line. About half of the sample members were aware of scholarships and other educational benefits to the poor, housing schemes and TRYSEM. Only a very few were aware of DWCRA, widow pension scheme, loans for artisans, conception Old Age Pension (OAP), loans for handicapped, grants for birth of girl children (first two children), grants for cremation expenses for SCs, and destitute person (Table 13.5).

Table 13.5: Perceptions of sample members

Name of the programme	*Percentage of members*			
	Aware	*Applied*	*Availed*	*Utilised*
IRDP	100	25	15	10
Marriage grant	80	10	10	10
Widow pension	25	–	–	–
Scholarship & other educational facilities	40	–	–	–
Housing facilities	45	–	–	–
Loans for artisans	15	20	15	15
TRYSEM	45	50	50	45
DWCRA	10	10	10	–
Conception grant	15	5	5	5
Sanitation facilities	15	–	–	–
Old age pension	20	–	–	–
Grant for girl children	15	5	5	–

TRYSEM programme has been accessed by half of the sample members, while a few of them have accessed IRDP, marriage grant, loan for artisans, DWCRA, conception grant and grant for girl children. Most of the sample members depended on SHARE and CHAD to obtain the benefits through government programmes. About half of the sample members did not face any difficulty in obtaining the programme. The rest faced problems such as difficulties in obtaining the necessary testimonials from the VAO or panchayat president, corruption, and delays in the sanction of the benefits.

Less than half the sample members followed up the programme at the government office and at the NGO by frequent visits or through middlemen who were either some commercial agents or the craft teachers of SHARE. More than half the sample members did not pay bribe while a few paid to the government officials and the commercial agents who mediated in the process.

A majority of the sample members who availed the programmes productively utilised the resources excepting the DWCRA beneficiaries. In the case of DWCRA beneficiaries, the revolving fund granted by the government was not put to use as the group members did not know for what purpose it should be used.

The government programme that is focused here is TRYSEM. This aims at providing income and employment to the beneficiaries. The beneficiaries here, the sample members, obtained training for craft activity on palm leaf and sisal fibre. The training has been made use of for income generation and employment. More than half the sample members utilised the accessed programme for income generation and employment purposes (Table 13.6). Before the training was obtained, they depended almost exclusively on agricultural labour which is seasonal and does not give sufficient income. After the training, the sample members stated that they got stable monthly income to meet their livelihood needs.

For approaching the government officials in the future 15 out of 20 of the sample members preferred to depend upon the NGO (Table 13.7). The sample members had a strong feeling that SHARE should be involved in every move of theirs. There was a mistaken notion among them that it was wrong to approach the government officials independently.

Table 13.6: Impact of the accessed programme

Particulars	*Total number of respondents*	*Percentage*
Income	10	50
Employment	1	5
Income and employment	1	5
Clearing debts and income	3	15
N.A.	5	25
Total	20	100

Table 13.7 : Dependency of the target group members in approaching government officials

Particulars	*Total number of respondents*	*Percentage*
Dependent on the NGO	15	75
Independent in approach	4	20
Dependent only for the time-being and can function independently in the long run	1	5
Total	20	100

CONCLUSION

SHARE realises that problems are bound to be there in creating and sustaining linkages with the government agencies. But, SHARE also realises that when there are enough and more number of programmes and funds available with these agencies, it is only fitting to adopt an attitude and approach which will require lot of patience and perseverance but which nevertheless are worthwhile, considering the benefits that will accrue to the target groups and the general population in terms of sustained development. By adopting such an attitude and approach SHARE is in a position even to identify the beneficiaries qualified to receive the benefits under the IRDP of the government and recommend them to the concerned block officials who have not so far rejected SHARE's recommendation in this regard. Looking positively, the linkages contributed to the following: (*i*) they helped in capacity building of the community; (*ii*) they have given SHARE a great learning experience; and (*iii*) they helped SHARE to gain recognition amongst government departments and officials in Vellore district and elsewhere. The linkages with NABARD and Women's Development Corporation have just begun. Hence, we conclude that in spite of having to face a few problems here and there, it is always useful and perhaps necessary for the NGO to make genuine attempts to enable the people to establish linkages with government agencies for the cause of the people and their total development.

Above all, mobilisation of funds from the government has so far been without much difficulty as the government officials have volunteered to do so. Support from Tamil Nadu Women's Development Corporation is purely voluntary. So is the third phase of TRYSEM training programme. This positive response from the government is mainly because SHARE is transparent, accountable, sincere and truly encourages people's participation. Hence, we feel that good governance within the organisation is an important factor that contributes to the linkages.

NOTE

1. The community Health and Development (CHAD) Programme of the Christian Medical College (CMC), Vellore, has been extending support services in health promotional activities. South India Producers' Association (SIPA), a member based organisation, has been helping SHARE in marketing its craft products.

14

Government Agencies and NGOs

Strategies Adopted by CRT in Tamil Nadu

T. SELWYN & P. SHOBANA

INTRODUCTION

The parent organisation for the Centre for Rural Technology (CRT) was Ketar Social Service Society, Nagercoil. CRT was registered in 1987 under the Trust Act by Mr. Joshua, who was the founder and Ex-Director. In the 1980s, the government was implementing the programmes on bio-gas, smokeless *chulha* and sanitation through the NGOs. In this context, the society branched out into two NGOs, CAT (Centre for Appropriate Technology) in Nagercoil and CRT in Tirunelvelli. CRT was basically formed to take up the government programmes, with the understanding that the government would implement the programme on bio-gas and smokeless *chulha* threugh the NGOs. The CRT began its work in Tirunelvelli which was one of the target areas of the government for the bio-gas project. The CRT took off as the pioneer NGO to implement the project as it fulfilled all the requirements as stated by the government, namely, the staff and the specialized personnel to carry over the project.

The overall objective of the organisation is to mobilise the resources from the government and work hand-in-glove with the government departments to help the poor and the needy people. The important activities of the NGO are: (*i*) construction of bio-gas plant, smokeless *chulha*, and latrines; and (*ii*) micro-finance programmes.

These activities are funded by the government and the donor agencies. Table 14.1 shows the quantum of funding received over a period of three years.

Table 14.1: Source-wise funding obtained by CRT

(*in Rupees*)

Source	*1995-96*	*1996-97*	*1997-98*
Government	365,447 (7)	280,306 (4.5)	146,666 (6.4)
Donor	4,706,225 (89.7)	5,099,925 (80.7)	1,173,310 (51.0)
Self & Bank Interest	172,458 (3.3)	936,921 (14.8)	979,214 (42.6)
Total	5,244,130 (100)	6,317,152 (100)	2,299,190 (100.0)

Note: The figures in parentheses denote column-wise percentages.

NOVIB, a Dutch co-financing agency, has been the major donor for the organisation. While the major portion of the funding was from the donor agencies there has been a gradual decrease in their contribution in the amount. This is basically due to the withdrawal strategy adopted by NOVIB. Such a policy has created a ground for the NGO to be self-reliant with the support extended by the donor. The organisation has so far not faced any problem with the donor agencies.

The activities of the NGO are undertaken by about 37 staff members under various projects. A large number of staff together with donor recommendation that the organisation should become sustainable resulted in two important developments. First, the NGO took initiative to form SHGs involved in micro-finance not only to branch out to different activities but also to have sustained contact with the people. As a part of this, the NGO has been working with women's groups under the community organisation programmes. The details of the group are given in Table 14.2. However, the organisation has contact with a large number of villages in the entire district, where they have been implementing appropriate technology programmes of the government. Second, the organisation seeks to become self-reliant through a corpus fund mobilised from the donor agency. There is, however, realisation that the real value of the corpus fund can only be increased through activities aimed at local resource mobilisation.

Table 14.2 : Progress of women's micro-finance groups

Year	*No. of villages*	*No. of groups*	*No. of target group members*
1996	25	25	750
1997	25	25	750
1998	30	30	750

The organisation has facilitated the linkage between the government departments and the people. The government schemes on the construction of bio-gas plant, smokeless *chulha* and latrines have been channelled to the people through the NGO. The continuous mobilisation of the government resources is an outcome of the effective implementation of the government programmes in the past; and the empowered people have mobilised the resources by themselves. The government has rightly depended on the NGO for its support in implementing the programme, as CRT is the only NGO, which is equipped with personnel required to implement the programmes relating to appropriate technology.

The NGO has been successful in mobilising the resources as it is the only NGO in the area interested in implementing the government programmes and this has forced the government to allocate the resources to the CRT. This, in a way, has made the government to thrust the responsibilities of the government on the CRT. This has also given rise to problems like

- delay in the release of funds;
- imposing the target at the end of the day which pressurises the work of the NGO; and
- *ad hocism* in demanding the reports on the programmes completed.

These problems have been overcome or handled by adopting various strategies. The NGO makes use of any meeting of NGOs or press meet to bring these problems to the limelight. The other strategies adopted are: addressing letters to the Collector directly by sending 'DO' letters regarding the delay in the release of funds by the concerned departments; and sometimes notifying that they propose to organise a *dharna*. These strategies have worked out on most occasions in getting the work done by the government officials.

Despite these problems, CRT has been successful in obtaining and implementing the programme for the following reasons. First, the organisation enjoys a monopoly status in the district as the only NGO having capacity to implement the programmes relating to appropriate technology. Second, the personal relationship with the Collector and the chief functionaries of the DRDA have also contributed to the continuous flow of funds from the government. The target group members are also accessing certain government programmes without the support of the NGO. This is mainly because of the membership of one of the target group members in the panchayat. The NGO has conducted mass awareness and training programmes on Panchayat Raj, and CRT staff have also participated in the canvassing of their target group members. The perception of the NGO on decentralised government is that the local decentralised government is the first entry point to monitor the proper implementation of government programmes and is also a proper channel to help the poor in accessing the government resources. The organisation, therefore, encourages the target group to contest in the elections for local decentralised government. One of the target group members contested and won the President post of a gram panchayat. Four members of the target group contested for the posts of ward members, and three of them won. In these gram panchayats, the target group of NGOs have an edge in so far as mobilisation of government resources is concerned.

In addition to the support of the target group members of the decentralized government, the NGO joins hands with other NGOs to address any immediate catastrophe or crises. This cannot certainly be called a well-knit network but the members gather together in a formal meeting to address any burning issue. The network has, however, not contributed to the development of the interface with the government.

Perceptions of the target group members

Twenty of the target group members belonging to three villages (Khazhaneerkulam, Muttukrishnaperi, Thayarthopu) of the CRT working area were interviewed to obtain their perception on the process adopted to access the government programmes. The sample members were beneficiaries of government programmes like TRYSEM, bio-gas plant, smokeless *chulha* and latrines. None of these programmes were under loan schemes.

Of the 20 samples members, 45 per cent were landless, while 40 per cent were marginal farmers. The rest were small farmers. All the sample members belong to backward castes. About 40 per cent of the sample have been members for more then four years, whereas 50 per cent were members for a period of less than two years.

The sample members were aware of the programmes like marriage grant, sanitation facilities, smokeless *chulha* and bio-gas, housing, drinking water, IRDP, maternity benefit, grant as deposit for two girl children, TRYSEM, Janata electricity, OAP/destitute pension, support for physically handicapped, tool-kits for artisans and scholarship for poor children. Among these programmes, a majority of the sample members were aware of programmes like marriage assistance, sanitation facilities, smokeless *chulas* and bio-gas, IRDP, maternity benefit and OAP/destitute pension. Most of the sample members had applied for sanitation facilities and smokeless *chulha* and had also availed the benefit. Almost all the sample members were utilising the benefits obtained except those who had certain infrastructure problems (Table 14.3). A majority of the sample members came to know about these programmes through the NGO. Only a few of them had come to know of the programme through villagers and panchayat.

Table 14.3: Government programmes—aware of, applied for and availed

Particulars	*Percentage of members*		
	Aware of the programmes	*Applying for the programme*	*Availing the programmes*
Marriage assistance	80	20	10
Sanitation	90	65	55
Smokeless Chulha/Bio-gas	95	75	75
Housing	15	–	–
Drinking water	15	15	–
IRDP	45	25	15
Maternity benefit	40	–	–
Girl children (grant)	25	–	–
TRYSEM	30	15	15
Janata electricity	10	5	5
OAP/destitute pension	40	5	–
Support for physically handicapped	30	10	5
Death compensation	15	5	–
Scholarship	25	5	5
Tool-kits for artisans	15	–	–

An interesting aspect that emerges from Table 14.3 is that there is a gap between the proportion of sample members aware of the programmes and the proportion of members eventually applying and availing the programmes. The gap is somewhat less in the case of sanitation, smokeless *chulha* and bio-gas. In the case of all other programmes, the proportion of members having awareness on them is less. The proportion of members availing these programmes is even less. This implies that the organisation has comparative advantages only in the case of programmes relating to appropriate technology.

The organisation has realised that there is need to build the capacity of the target group in accessing individual beneficiary oriented programmes. Since the organisation is in the forefront in mobilising the programmes relating to appropriate technology for the people, they do not actively participate in the interface process. For instance, a majority (80 per cent) of the sample members had not met the government officials at all either on their own or with the help of CRT staff. The rest approached with the help of CRT staff. Naturally, there was no follow-up on the part of the target group. Nearly half of them had not bothered about any follow-up to the applications that they had submitted to the government. The rest of the members sought to enquire about the status of their applications at CRT's office.

Because the NGO was in the forefront to mobilise the resources the target group could access them without facing any difficulties. Only 10 per cent of them had reported that they had to face delays and pay bribe to the officials. One of the target group members could not avail the programme as she did not have sufficient money for payment towards the margin component (Table 14.4.).

Table 14.4: Problems faced in obtaining the resources

Particulars	*Total no. of respondents*	*Percentage*
Financial problem	1	5
Infra-structure problem	1	5
Delay	1	5
Delay and bribe	1	5
No problems	16	80
Total	20	100

It is, therefore, not surprising that a majority of the members stated that they depended on the NGO to obtain the resources. They also stated that they would continue to depend on NGO in the future. (Table 14.5). The NGO is considered as a provider, helper, guide by the sample members.

Table 14.5 : Do members have the capacity to approach government officials independently?

Particulars	*Total no. of respondents*	*Percentage*
Can approach individually	7	35
Can approach but need CRT support	2	10
Cannot approach at all	11	55
Total	20	100

CONCLUSION

CRT respects the linkage with the government programme. The government has a number of programmes to be implemented for the people and are bound to do so. In this process, the organisation is collaborating and implementing the programmes. If there is good rapport between these two actors in the execution of the programme, any programme can be successful. The government agencies should be free of biased and malpractices and should take care to involve genuine and sincere NGOs for the success of its programme. On its part, the organisation needs to build the capacity of the people to approach the government officials on their own, and access the programmes meant for them.

Index